Riga & its b

Published by
Landmark Publishing Ltd,
Ashbourne Hall, Cokayne Avenue, Ashbourne, Derbyshire DE6 1EJ England
Tel: (01335) 347349 Fax: (01335) 347303 e-mail: landmark@clara.net

2nd Edition
ISBN 1 84306-096-5

British Library Cataloguing in Publication Data: a catalogue record for this
book is available from the British Library.

Print: Gutenberg Press Ltd, Malta
Editor: Kay Coulson
Cartography: James Allsopp
Design: Samantha Witham

Front cover: Aerial view of Riga
Back cover: Looking down Brivibas Boulevard to the Freedom Monument

Picture Credits

Riga 800: Front cover, 61 both
Riga Dome: Back cover, 21, 27, 28,
32, 53, 81, 89, 93B, 149B, 153B, 157B
Juris Krumins, Presidential Office:
4, 80BL, 121
**Jurmala Spa & Tourism
Information Centre:** 5, 12, 13, 64,
69B, 72, 76/7, 80T, 80BL, 148, 149T, 153T
Riga Motor Museum: 8, 92
**Museum of Decorative
& Applied Art:** 9, 20, 93T, 96
Georg Baumanis: 17, 37, 40, 52B,
48, 49, 84, 160/1
Irena Bakula: 41
Riga Castle: 52T
Small Guild: 55, 56/57 all, 156/7
Jurmala Dome: 68T
Kemeri National Parks: 68B, 69T
Inta Ruka: 86

Anita Zabilevska: 88B
Edmunds Lucis: 88T
**Museum of History of Riga
& Navigation:** 97 both
Rundale Palace Museum: 100,
104/5, 109TL&TR
Araisi Museum: 109
David Hopkinson: 112
Mary Evans Picture Library: 128
**Mary Evans/Sigmund
Alexander Meledin:** 119
R Skrabaus: 129
Latvian National Opera: 132/3
Steve J Sherman: 136
**J Audrey Ellison, International
Artists' Management:** 137
Peter Jönsson AB: 138

LANDMARK VISITORS GUIDE

Riga
& its beaches

Farrol Kahn

Farrol Kahn is a journalist and has written several books on
aviation medicine. He lives in Oxford where he heads
The Aviation Health Institute.

Acknowledgements

The author would like to thank the numerous people and institutions who have made the writing of this book possible.

It began with the Ministry of Culture and the Latvian Tourism Development Agency. Karina Pétersone, Minister of Culture was an enthusiastic supporter of the initiative and in spite of her busy schedule wrote a splendid foreword to the book.

Anda Rezgale and later Aivars Kalnins opened many doors for me and have been most generous with their time and help at the Tourist Office.

I was fortunate in meeting Vaira Vike-Freiberga before her election as President of the Republic of Latvia when she was the Director of the Latvian Institute and assisted me with the national cultural treasure of Dainas of which she is the world authority. To her I am extremely grateful.

At the London Latvian Embassy I would like to thank H E Normans Penke, Eva Staltmane, Irena Hamilton and Juris Bone.

There are many others to whom I am specially grateful: Knuts Skujenieks, Janis Borgs, Oliver Staas, Solveiga Freiberga, Paul Taylor, Dale Lawrence, Natalya Krasnopeyeve, Inguna Bakuradze, Ineta Petersone, Vita Jermolovica, Ilze Martinsone, Ieva Lesinska, Anda Vilka, Leva Iltnere, Inta Ruka, Anita Zabilevska, Gatins Kokins, Juris Kapralis, Irena Bakule, Vilnis Smits, Mairita Brice, Liga Libarte, Sarah Bruce Jones, Lilita Laine, Raimonds Auskaps, Neil Taylor, Arija Vanaga, Julia and Maud Rosenthal.

• CONTENTS •

Left: The author, left, with the President of the Republic of Latvia, Vaira Vike-Freiberga

Opposite: Sunbathers enjoying the Jurmala sunshine

LANDMARK VISITORS GUIDE

Riga
& its beaches

Farrol Kahn

Latvian Economy

1. How successful has the unwinding of the economy been from the former Soviet regime?

What difficulties have been encountered? Have these been resolved?

Implementation of consistent reform policy since regaining of independence has resulted in the creation of functioning liberal and open market economy in Latvia. Substantial macroeconomic stability has been achieved – low inflation, stable national currency, robust economic

Mr Ilmars Rimsevic
Governor
Bank of Latvia

growth rates, low government debt and fiscal deficit and healthy financial sector. The forthcoming accession to the EU and NATO reflects the tremendous progress Latvia has achieved during the last decade.

2. How fast has the economy grown since Independence?

During the first years of independence country experienced contraction of output as Latvia had to implement challenging reforms and overcome shocks stemming form the change of economic system. In the mid-1990s Latvia entered a period of recovery. Since 1997 Latvia reported the highest GDP growth rates amongst the other EU member and candidate countries – in the period between 1997 and 2002, Latvia's GDP grew by 36.8% or by 6.1% on average per annum. Last year GDP grew by 6.1%. Rapid economic growth has been achieved in a low inflation environment.

3. How fast does he expect the economy to grow once Latvia is part of the European Union?

Will joining the European Union accelerate the growth of the economy?

Latvia's economic growth will be positively affected by the EU membership. Annual GDP growth in the medium term is expected to equal to about 5-7%. Latvia will benefit from more effective conditions for the trade with the EU, from the increasing capital base and improving infrastructure resulting from EU structural funds, inflow of foreign investment, reduction of risk factors and improvement of overall business environment. The accession to the EMU and associated nominal and real convergence with the EMU will also bring further ground for sustainable development.

4. What are the fastest growing industries? Will they also grow in the European Union? What new industries are expected to grow once Latvia joins the European Union?

What are the expectations of the industrial sector once Latvia is part of the European Union?

Manufacturing, construction, trade and commercial services are currently the fastest growing industries. It is expected that accession to the EU and associated improvement in business climate will positively influence economic development. We expect that Latvia will be able to withstand the increasing competition, as during the last years Latvian economy already has been very open, and liberal economic policy has been pursued.

5. Labour costs are low at present. Will they grow once Latvia is in the European Union as they have done in Hungary?

Labour costs in Latvia remain rather low and competitive from the investors' point of view. Further development of labour costs will be largely determined by development of productivity and output. Our current experience suggests that productivity growth outstrips wage growth therefore competitiveness is preserved.

6. Should Latvia's economic performance always be linked to Lithuania and Estonia even in the European Union? How will Latvia's economy compare with the two other Baltic states?

Deepening of regional economic cooperation with the neighbouring Baltic States is characteristic feature of last years. The Current share of Estonia and Lithuania in Latvia's foreign trade turnover reaches 15.1%.

There have been periods or spheres where one or another Baltic country has developed more or less successfully. However all in all economic development goals, trends and situation in all three Baltic countries are quite similar. Currently Latvia presents the highest economic growth rates in the region.

7. The usual facts and figures about the Latvian economy would be appreciated e.g. GNP, average wage etc.

Main macroeconomic indicators of Latvia

	2000	2001	2002
GDP, %	6.8	7.9	6.1
GDP per capita, USD	3024	3254	3596
Inflation, %	2.6	2.5	1.9
Unemployment, %	7.8	7.7	7.6
Average gross wage, USD	247	253	280
Growth of exports, %	12.2	11.1	12.1
Growth of imports, %	12.2	13.8	13.4
Budget deficit, % of GDP	-2.8	-1.8	-2.5
Government external debt, % of GDP	8.0	9.5	9.1
Government 5 -year bond yield, %	8.93	8.06	5.5
Interest rate for long term credits in lats, %	10.3	10.4	8.7

INTRODUCTION

Riga is a rare discovery in a world that is rapidly running out of new destinations and I certainly did not set out to find such a place, as Robert Byron did in his quest for Oxiana. My father had come from a nearby town, Jelgava (which was then known as Mitau), and I had embarked on a trip to find my roots at the suggestion of a friend.

The city had 'hidden itself', first under the Russian and then under the Soviet sphere of influence, until the last century when Latvia attained Independence for two decades from 1918 to 1940. However, through the secret Molotov-Ribbentrop Pact of August 23rd, 1939, the country was assigned to the Soviet Union and occupied until the early nineties.

During the sensitive period of Perestroika, the Prime Minister of the UK, John Major, played a significant role in ensuring that the Baltic States gained independence, according to a former Latvian ambassador to the Soviet Union, Janis Peters.

On a visit to Moscow, John Major committed a breach of Protocol by first inviting the three representatives from Estonia, Latvia and Lithuania to a meeting before seeing President Gorbachov. He sounded them on their views of Independence and when they affirmed their strong interest, he pushed the Soviet Union to acknowledge their constitutional rights. Formal recognition took place on 24th August, 1991. However, for most people in the West, Latvia does not exist or at a guess they would indicate it is part of the Russian republic, which is a great shame and loss to them.

Tacitus was the first to put the country on the map for the Romans when he wrote about the people in his ethnographical work, Germania. He had little to say about these Latvian tribes, who were closer to the Prussians with whom they shared the Indo-European language, but it was startling enough.

The Gulf of Riga he described as a tame, stagnant body of water with a resemblance to parts of the Mediterranean. It marked an important boundary of the earth, because of the phenomenon of the midnight sun which provided a brilliance, that according to him, even dimmed the stars.

He called the people the Aestii, and praised them for their diligence and determination, compared to the indolent Germans who did not cultivate their crops with the same zeal. The Aestii or the Balts were distinguished from other tribes because they were the only people who harvested glaesum or amber from the sea. But as barbarians, they never understood its ornamental worth nor did they enquire about its origins. The Romans had of course, and even burnt the fossil gum to test its properties.

Riga is a place that Pushkin dreamt of visiting as his greatest love, Anna Petrovna Kern, resided there with her husband. It was the period when his infatuation for her turned into a powerful passion and he desperately longed to be with her. But the Tsar, who had exiled him to his estate at Mikhailovskoe, had forbidden travel to the city. Instead, Pushkin cooled his heels and wrote his best love poem, *K*.

In the early 1800s, Riga was on the provincial music circuit in Central Europe and Richard Wagner spent two seminal years in the city. When he left he was determined to stop this itinerant lifestyle, partly caused by fleeing from creditors and had conceived the grandiose idea of Bayreuth, which would be supported by a wealthy patron.

Johann Gottfried von Herder, the German poet and philosopher had a brief sojourn in the city.

In the 1930s it was the place to hang around if you were interested in communists and spies or both, as it was the window to the Soviet Union. George Kennan from the US State Department was here as was the author Graham Greene who was credited with calling it 'Parisian' or 'Paris of the North'. John F Kennedy also turned up as a twenty-two year-old student just before the World War II and there is a plaque on the house he stayed in at 22 Ausekla Street.

From a cultural focal point, Riga has produced leading figures like the film director, Sergei Eisenstein, the philosopher, Isaiah Berlin, the US philanthropist Joseph Hirshhorn and the ballet star, Mikhail Baryshnikov. The city is a cocktail of architectural styles from crusader castles to Renaissance; Gothic cathedrals and Classicism; to the finest examples of Art Nouveau which few Westerners have seen as they have been omitted from reference books. The latter have now been added to Unesco's World Cultural Heritage List.

There always has been a strong British connection since the eighteenth century, mostly through trade. One of the best mayors, George Armistead's forebears came from Yorkshire. More recently the BBC Proms commissioned Peteris Vasks to write a symphony. Football star Marian Pahar was recruited to play for Southampton and top coach Gary Johnson, from Watford, now manages the Latvian National Team.

Hedonists also have a wide choice of activities from beaches to night clubs. The beach coastline, which stretches over 25 miles (40km) and in parts resembles the wild African coast because of the lack of high-rise hotel development, with trees growing near the waterline, has been recommended by no less a figure than the poet, Osip Mandelstam. 'It is famed for its oozy, pure yellow and astonishingly fine sand (even in an hourglass one could hardly find such sand!)' he exclaimed in what could appear to be as inadvertent advertising copy.

While you lie on this 'yellow finely milled canary sand,' no pesky beach salesperson will accost you out of your holiday reverie, and if you walk long enough you will find the only ice-cream cart vendor. There are amazing examples of wooden dachas all over the coast, including the most recent little masterpiece of the top German architect, Meinhard von Gerkan.

Sybarites will find satisfaction at the several spa hotels where they can indulge in mud baths and mineral water massages. The night club scene is as sophisticated as the Parisian Moulin Rouge and caters for all ages, including teeny boppers. An added inducement is that the city is celebrated for the special beauty of its girls who tend to be fashioned like top models, but statuesque and they outnumber the men by two to one.

The food and beer will also excite the palate as there is a latter-day Conran on site and a surprising number of good restaurants. Forget Munich or Prague for the beerfest and come here to try the range of ales in a city where they are so good that you can drink them between courses instead of wine. You can also try Stalin's preferred beer, Rigas Originalais, which incidentally has a very bitter aftertaste.

I never did find traces of our family in Jelgava, because I discovered this Parisian city instead. As a new destination for the twenty-first century, Riga is second to none. It has sea, sun, sand, culture, music, art and is the repository of about three million Dainas or folk songs. And it is cheap. What more can one expect from a capital city.

General

Riga, which is the capital of Latvia, is situated at the south-eastern extremity of the Gulf of Riga in 57°3'N, 24°1'E, with a cosmopolitan population of some 900,000 comprising forty-seven per cent Russians, thirty-eight per cent Latvians, nine per cent Belarussians and Ukranians, and two per cent Poles. The city extends to both banks of the Daugava River, and like Paris there is a right bank where the old town of Vecriga is and a left bank, the Pardaugava, with the tall television tower.

History

Latvia was unknown to Europe until 1158 when Bremen Merchants on a trading mission to Wisby in Gotland Island were shipwrecked on the Gulf of Riga near the mouth of the Daugava River. They formed a settlement on the sandy peninsula between the Daugava and its small tributary the Ridzene from which Riga derives its name. The river was filled in over a century ago although the river bed is still visible.

The Middle Ages

In 1201, Bishop Albert who had come to convert the inhabitants to Christianity founded the town and made it the seat of the Bishop of Livonia according to the chronicle of Henricus Livonicus. He established a colony with German settlers, established the Dome School in 1211, and founded the Crusader Order of the Brothers of the Sword which joined with the Teutonic Order of Prussia in 1237, known as the Livonian Order.

Riga acquired great privileges and possessions and in 1282 joined the Hanseatic League, adopting the Hamburg code before the end of the thirteenth century. There was constant friction between the archbishops, citizens and knights, which sometimes resulted in pitched battles in which the two former parties united against the third, that generally maintained the upper hand.

As the city grew in prosperity, Guilds were established in 1330 for craftsmen and merchants. In 1522 Riga embraced the tenets of the Reformation and in 1541 joined the League of Schmalkalden. The first library was founded in 1524 and the first play, *The Prodigal Son* by a Rigan poet Valdis Burhatds, was performed.

Changing rulers

In 1561, the Livonian Order under its last Grand Master, Gothard Kettler, ceded the country to Poland as they could no longer withstand the Russian attacks and in return Kettler received the Duchy of Courland or Kurzeme (see entry: Rundale). Some twenty years later, the Polish King Stepan Bathory, conquered the city as it had been given an independent status by the previous Grand Master, Walter Plettenberg. Catholicism was reinstated and the Gregorian Calendar introduced that led to Calendar riots in which two of the ringleaders were beheaded. In 1588 the first book was printed in Riga and the Latvian School established in St Jacob's Church.

During the wars between Poland and Sweden, Riga was captured by the Swedish King, Gustavus Adolfus, on September 15th 1621 after a protracted siege that lasted six weeks. Swedish rule which extended for 88 years was termed a golden period because Latvian culture was encouraged, resulting in the publication of the Bible, books and a dictionary in their language. The Bible was translated by a Lutheran Pastor, Ernst Glück, from a grant by the Swedish Administration.

Russian rule

The town was unsuccessfully besieged by Tsar Alexey Mikhailovich in 1656 but the Russians returned in 1709 and the town which had suffered from severe flooding and later, starvation in which two thirds of the inhabitants had died, surrendered on July 4th, 1710 to Count Sheremetyev. The Count had earlier taken as prisoners Ernst Glück and his family, including his adopted daughter Marta Skrovronska who later married Peter the Great and became Catherine I. The Russian occupation of the town and country was the longest of all foreign powers and continued until 1918.

Nineteenth century – visitors' views

At the beginning of the nineteenth century, a couple of visitors made interesting comments on the city. 'As soon as you drive into Riga,' said Nikolay Karamzin, the Russian historian, 'you will see it as a merchants' city – many shops, many people, the river full of different

Opposite: View from hotel terrace, Majori beach
Below: Yachts moored on the Lielupe River, Jurmala

Lord Lawson's Latvian background

"The only member of my family to have come from Latvia was my father's father, originally Gustav Leibson." said Lord Lawson of Blaby, former Chancellor of the Exchequer in the UK Thatcher government. "His family was part of the sizeable German-speaking Jewish community which flourished in Riga in the nineteenth century. His elder brother, Herman Leibson, graduated in medicine from Derpt (Tartu) University, and subsequently practised as a country doctor in northern Latvia, initially in the village of Karpogori. He later moved to Pinega, where his son, Lev Leibson, was born (in 1900), later to become Professor Leibson, the founder of comparative endocrinology in Russia and, in his later years, one of the acknowledged doyens of Russian physiology. Most of the Leibsons subsequently left Latvia for Russia, settling first in Archangel and then in St Petersburg. I am not aware of any remaining in Latvia."

"Meanwhile, towards the end of the nineteenth century, Herman Leibson's younger brother, Gustav, after leaving school, decided not to go to university but to seek his fortune in America. The plan was to take the steamer from Riga to London, and then sail from London to New York. In the event, almost by accident, he settled in London, where my father was born (1904). When Gustav entered my father for Westminster School (a well-known public school, where both my father and I were educated) during World War I, when anti-German feeling was rife, the school advised him to change the family name from the Germanic Leibson to Lawson, which he did."

nations' ships, and the Stock Exchange is so packed, there is no room to turn around'.

Another visitor, B V Pestelis, complained about how expensive Riga was, as did Karamzin. He warned other male visitors to be careful when meeting a woman on the street, as it was difficult to distinguish between servants and ladies, because everyone was well dressed. He also wondered at the selection of food which came from all parts of the world. There was wine from Africa, sugar from America, grapes from Astrakhan, port and cheese from England and venison from Poland and Russia.

During the Crimean War the English fleet under Admiral Sir Charles Napier blockaded the town in 1854. In 1857 the fortifications were demolished and reconstruction of the city began which would result in its population increasing sevenfold from some 70,000 to 500,000 by the beginning of the twentieth century.

Riga also became the most important city for science and

technology in Russia and the site for the production of railway carriages, cars, aircraft and bicycles.

There was a wave of nationalism that resulted in the formation of the Latvian National Awakening movement launched by Krisjanis Valdemars, Juris Alunans and Krisjanis Barons who in 1862 also founded the 'Newspaper of St Petersburg'. The Baltic Germans, a minority who ran the country saw the newspaper as a threat to their power base and persuaded the Russians to shut it down. In 1868 the Latvian Society was established and in 1873, the first song festival took place in Riga which promoted the development of the Latvian culture.

Twentieth century changes

On January 13th, 1905 there were demonstrations in the city during which seventy people were shot by troops. During the World War I, when Riga was occupied by the Germans, the Russians and the Bolsheviks, and the Latvian Riflemen proved to be a formidable fighting unit, the Latvians saw their first chance of Independence and established the State on November 18th, 1918. On January 26th, 1921 after fighting for Independence for three years Latvia was acknowledged by European nations and admitted to the League of Nations the same year. Over the next two decades many things happened in Riga.

A new currency, the lat, was issued and Janis Cakste was elected the President. The first bus routes and taxis appeared, Radio Latvia started broadcasts and the Ethnographic Museum opened. The Freedom Monument and the

Brother's Cemetery were built and the conversion of the five Zeppelin Hangars into the Central Market, the most modern market in Europe, was completed.

The city was relatively prosperous during the two decades between the two World Wars; this was partly due to the authoritarian regime of Prime Minister Karlis Ulmanis who was able to take strong measures in the years of economic depression.

In 1939, due to the secret non-aggression pact between Russia and Germany, the Soviet Union forced upon Latvia a treaty of mutual assistance which amounted to an annexation. Under the Molotov-Ribbentrop agreement all the Baltic Germans left the country. During the World War II, Riga was 'liberated' three times, twice by the Soviets, in 1940 and 1944 and once by the Nazis in 1941. An estimated 600,000 people, a third of the pre-war population perished or disappeared in mass deportations.

After the war, Riga became multicultural as industrial production was increased and workingmen were brought in from all over the Soviet Union.

Independence

The road to the country's Independence began again in the late 1980's. In 1987, on June 14th, protests against the 1941 deportations to Siberia took place at the Freedom Monument. The following year on June 1st, the 1939 Molotov-Ribbentrop agreement was denounced at the Latvian Writers Union Conference. On November 11, the Latvian flag was flown from Riga Castle. On August 23rd 1989, a human chain of over two million

Latvians, Estonians and Lithuanians stretched from Tallinn to Riga and Vilnius to protest the fiftieth anniversary of the Molotov-Ribbentrop agreement which gave the three republics to the USSR.

A year later, on March 18th, the Latvian Popular Front Party wins elections and on May 4th, the Supreme Council adopted the Declaration of Independence. In 1991, from January 13th to 27th, barricades were set up, outside the house of parliament and around the old town, which were manned twenty-four hours a day. On January 20th, Soviet Special Forces OMON attacked and occupied the Ministry of Interior building and killed seven people. Almost eight months later Independence was again achieved in the twentieth century on August 23rd and acknowledged by the USSR on 24th.

On July 8th 1999, the first woman President Vaira Vike-Freiberga was elected. A year earlier, she had been Professor of Psychology at the University of Montreal. 'This is an important hour,' she said in her acceptance speech. 'We open a new page in the history of Latvia.'

Architectural development

Vecriga, the old town, still preserves it Hanseatic features – high storehouses, with spacious granaries and cellars, flanking the narrow winding streets. The only open spaces are the marketplace and two other squares.

Medieval times

The medieval Riga was a typical city-state with its rural suburbs which developed close to the city walls around the fourteenth century. The city walls were surrounded by moats, as was the castle, which was outside the walls. There were bastions which were interspersed with ravelins to offer advantage to the city when attacked. (See engraving of M Merian in 1638, Museum of History of Riga and Navigation.)

Until the sixteenth century suburbs around the city were illegal and were frequently destroyed by the Town Council. It was at the behest of the Polish King, Stefan Batory, when the city was ruled by the Polish-Lithuanian alliance, that the first legal suburbs appeared in the 1580s. There was the proviso that the houses were to be built out of timber without cellars and at a sufficient distance from the city walls.

These grew alongside the two main trade routes, the southern towards Russia and the north-eastern along the gulf to Estonia. Few antiquities of the medieval town remain. The oldest church, The Dom (St Mary's) established in 1215, was burned in 1547 and the present building dates from the late 1500s but has been restored since 1883.

St Peter's Church with its beautiful tower 412ft (126m) high was erected in 1406-9. The castle which was built in 1494-1515 by the Master of the Knights of The Livonian Order, Walter von Plettenberg, is a spacious building often rebuilt. The House of the Blackheads, a club of foreign merchants was founded in 1330, and the Dutch renaissance gable was added in 1620. However, it was damaged during the last war and has been restored. The Livlandisch Ritterhaus, a former

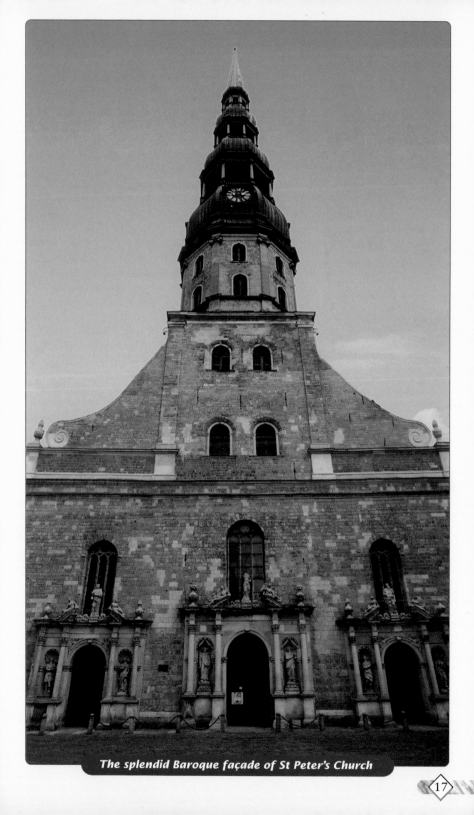

The splendid Baroque façade of St Peter's Church

meeting place for the Livonian nobility no longer exists.

In the sixteenth century the suburbs were inhabited by local peasants and artisans. According to Irena Bakule, The Inspector for Heritage Protection of Riga, a panorama of Riga demonstrates the suburban area sprinkled with farmsteads, one- or two-roomed wooden houses built from horizontal logs with gabled roofs and covered with thatch and scattered alongside roads.

Up to the middle of the nineteenth century, the ancient city of Riga was a fortress enclosed by ramparts, fortified walls and moats. The suburbs had a regular gridiron street layout and blocks divided into large parcels with houses on the streets and orchards with vegetable gardens in the inner area.

Nineteenth-century development

When Napoleon attacked Russia in 1812, the Governor of the city ordered that the suburbs be burned in case of an invasion. It proved to be a false alarm but after the great fire the Russian influence in the rebuilding of the houses was strong and the Classical style for the façades was made compulsory. This regulation also applied to new building in Riga. By the middle of the century, there was rapid development of industry which tended to supplant orchards in the inner space of the blocks and changed the rural character.

As Riga grew the population increased and so did the traffic on the roads out of the Vecriga. There was little space to build new houses or ease the congestion on the roads.

The only solution was to expand beyond the city walls as the alternative was untenable, wooden houses in the suburbs which could be burnt down during a siege.

The Town Council approached Governor-General, Prince Alexander Suvorov and a petition was taken to St Petersburg. In due course, Tsar Alexander II agreed to give permission for the fortifications to be pulled down on November 15 1857. A special ceremony was held to mark the occasion in which the Mayor and the Prince were among the first to thrust a spade into the soil. (The spade is still on display in the Riga Museum of History and Navigation.) The demolition work was carried out for the next six years.

Building of the boulevards

A master plan by architects Johann Felsko and Otto Dietze had been approved earlier and the surrounding area was reconstructed according to their plans. The old moat was converted into a canal with gardens and the esplanade was replaced by a semi-circle of boulevards, enclosing the old city, with many public buildings. A large part of the earthworks was carried away and piled up where the sand bastion had stood to create a man-made hill now called Bastion Hill. Coincidentally, a similar process was begun in Vienna when the ramparts that girdled the old town were removed in 1858-60 and replaced by a magnificent boulevard, the Ringstrasse, which was two miles (3.2km) long and lined with trees, splendid buildings and monuments.

New boulevards were formed along both banks of the canal

which is now connected with the Daugava River, providing a steady flow. On the old city side, Kronvalda Boulevard, which forms the border of Kronvalda Park, runs first into Basteja and then into Aspazijas Boulevard. The new boulevard on the suburban side has Kalpaka which also borders Krovalda Park and Boulevard Raina runs parallel to Basteja and Aspazijas. (Of course at the time, they were named after the Russian royal family. Street name changes are a common occurrence in the city. From 1919 to 1939, names were changed sixteen times but the record year was in 1923 when 151 streets were renamed). Brivibas or Freedom had previous incarnations as Great Sand, Alexander, Lenin, Revolution and for the shortest period, Adolf Hitler.

The thrust outside the walls and the moats towards the suburbs was a precursor to a splendid architectural style that would radically change the city's face from heavy, gloomy Swedish, Germanic and Russian building to the lighter, sophisticated western influences found for example in Paris; hence its nickname in the thirties 'Paris of the North' or 'Little Paris'. However, with the development of the boulevard semicircle came the Eclectic style of stately residences and imposing public buildings; the Opera House, the French Embassy, the National Theatre with its Neo-Renaissance façade, the Riga City Council and the State Museum of Art. It is an outstanding example of town planning in the nineteenth century.

Another important element of the Felsko and Dietze project, was to create green space. The Board of Parks, which was established in 1879, was headed by Georg Kuhfalt who undertook the reconstruction and design of the city's gardens and parks for thirty-five years until 1914. He introduced exotic plants and shrubs and bow-shaped paths, one of which ran behind the National Theatre and is called the Alley of Love.

The twentieth century

At the turn of the century, Riga experienced rapid growth with the population almost doubling to half a million during the course of fifteen years, from 1899 to 1914. Construction now spread far beyond the two bands of semi-circular boulevards towards Tallina Street, encompassing some eleven streets to the north east. The two-floored wooden models of classicism were replaced by apartment blocks with shops on the ground floor.

The earliest examples of Art Nouveau architecture appeared in Riga in 1899 and were designed by Alfred Aschenkampff for A Grasset's commercial and apartment house at 7 Audeju Street in the heart of the old town *(see page 61)* and Rudolf Zirkwitz's apartment house at 11 Vilandes Street. This should be compared with another building built a year later in Jurmala, 58 Strelnieku Avenue (lit 3) in which similar geometrical designs were used on the walls.

The highlight of any visit to Riga is the Art Nouveau architecture. There are over 200 buildings in the new city and some forty sprinkled in the old town. Although prime examples of the architecture are found in cities like Brussels, Paris, Munich and Vienna, none have *(c ont'd on page 22)*

• ART NOUVEAU •

To signal the beginning of a new century, Art Nouveau was born. It was a rebellion against eclecticism, that mixture of historical styles, and introduced a contemporary, modern artistic approach based on the concept of turning useful into beautiful. Form follows function. 'Forms emerge from forms and others arise or descend from these. All are related, interwoven, intermeshed, interconnected, interblended... They sway and swirl and mix and drift interminably. They shape, they reform, they dissipate' (Such a description by the US architect Louis Sullivan will suffice to describe this new movement that evolved differently in many countries in the late nineteenth century.)

The 'New Art' movement had a universal appeal. It stimulated linear austerity from Charles Rennie Mackintosh in Glasgow; the steel sinuosities of Victor Horta in Brussels; the chequer-board geometries of Josef Hoffmann in Vienna; Louis Sullivan's vegetal grammar of ornament in Chicago; Antoni Gaudi's eye catching biomorphic surfaces and undulating walls in Barcelona and Mikhail Eisenstein's spectacular operetta of façades in Riga.

The architectural language was characterised as Jugendstil or Youth Style in Germany, Secession in Austria, Eel Style in Belgium and Floral, Noodle or Macaroni Style in Italy, Modernista in Spain and Style Metro in France. But the form of expression was not limited to buildings, it extended to furniture, jewels, paintings, posters, glass, china, clothing, tableware, books, wallpaper and applied arts.

Among the well-known names were Paul Gaugin, Gustav Klint, James Whistler, Henri Toulouse-Lautrec, Edward Munch, Alphonse Mucha and Aubrey Beardsley in painting and posters; Louis Tiffany, Rosenthal, Renee Lalique, Georg Jensen, Liberty and Carlo Bugatti in ornaments and Worth and Paul Poiret in fashion.

In Riga, Art Nouveau found full expression after the city's 700th anniversary exhibition of Industry and Crafts (see The Tale of Two Majors). 'This taste developed especially after the Anniversary Exhibition of 1901, and it was something new indeed' wrote the Latvian art critic Janis Asars at the time.

*Opposite: "The Swimmer" by Stafans Bercs (1893-1961).
Private collection*

Above: One of Eisenstein's masterpieces

such an outstanding collection concentrated in a small area, nor the erotic content eg. 93 Brivibas Street. Many of the houses are in good repair and there are excellent illustrations in Professor Janis Krastins's book, *The Art Nouveau Architecture of Riga*, where he refers to the style as 'music in stone'. I confess that I did not immediately respond to these melodies because I prefer the simpler works of Art Deco. However, after several visits I found the sounds appealing.

Fine façades run along Alberta and Kalku Streets and for aficionados I should mention there are several distinctions of style. Kenins School at 15/17 Terbatas Street illustrates the National Latvian Romanticism that broke out after bloody clashes with Tsarist troops in 1905.

Then there is the perpendicular style of which Janis Gailis's shops and apartment building at 13 Terbatas Street is an example. If you want to take in as many variations of the theme as possible, walk down Smilsu Street. For the record there are seven types including decorative, eclectic, perpendicular, rationalism, national romanticism and gothic revival *(see Walking Tours)*.

A cornucopia of diverse Art Nouveau items other than building can be found in the Riga Museum of History and Navigation *(see separate entry)*.

Business in Riga

Latvia has always been a trading zone between east and west from earliest times, when amber was an important product to barter, to the

Art Nouveau Designer

Mikhail Eisenstein, the father of the Russian film director, was a leading exponent of the eclectic decoration with his amazing designs that combine ornamental motifs from cast cement, ceramics, metal and timber. The top of the frontage of the apartment housed at 2 Alberta Street with its round windows open to the sky is both dramatic and reminds one of the film sets of buildings that were later used by American studios. He was undoubtedly a genius with his designs.

There was little love lost between father and son and Sergei was dismissive and cutting about the buildings. He called him 'a maker of cakes' and urged his friends 'to look at the cream on that house's face'.

'Father, who placed statues of human beings one and a half storeys high, stretched out as a decoration, on the corners of the houses. Father, who deployed women's arms, made from iron drainpipes and with gold rings in their hands, beneath the angle of the roof. In bad weather, it was fun watching the rain stream down between their tin legs. Father, who triumphantly entwined in the sky the tails of the plaster lions – *lions de plâtre* – which were piled up on the rooftops. Father himself was a *lion de plâtre*. And he bequeathed to me an unhealthy passion for winding layer upon layer – which I tried to sublimate into a fascination for Catholic Baroque and the over-elaborate work of the Aztecs.'

most recent. The Roman historian Tacitus was complimentary about their diligence as farmers, fishermen and gatherers of glass or amber in the sea, compared to the warlike Germans who showed their characteristic carelessness towards such matters.

Professor Arnis Radins of the History Museum of Latvia mentions that they were good businessmen during the early Iron Age (1AD to 400AD). 'There is evidence that Latvians had trading contacts with all the surrounding territories, particularly the south Baltic', he said. 'They also played a mediator role as many objects from the east and south-west, the Vistula, Niemen and Dnieper, passed through Latvia to Estonia and Finland'.

Trade

During the Middle Ages, Bremen merchants were the first to visit their settlements and take their products back to Germany and Western Europe. When the Hanseatic towns were formed, Riga became a prominent member. Under the Swedes, it became the largest city in Sweden and later, under the Tsars, it was the second largest commercial city.

According to John Murray's travel handbook in 1865, some 2,000 ships loaded goods: grain, linseed, flax, hemp and wood for export – and imports included salt, herrings, coal, iron, machinery and other goods.

Manufacturing

At the beginning of the twentieth century, Riga was a bustling metropolis and manufacturing industries like the Russian motor industry, textiles, railway carriages and chemicals were located there. Such a position of technological progress was maintained throughout the Soviet era with high-tech industries, e.g. electronics, established in the country.

Banking

One of the youngest top bankers in Central Europe, Valerijs Kargins, would agree that Latvia is now a country of great opportunities. 'There is access to the Soviet economy through acquisitions,' he said.

He is president of Parex Bank, which is the largest in Latvia in terms of assets and capital and controls some twenty-five per cent of the total of core banking services with an authorised capital of $70 million. Together with the Unibank, the Hansa bank, the Rietumu and Latvijas Krajbanka, it accounts for sixty-one per cent of the sector's assets. They grew through acquiring the oldest Russian bank, the Nobles Livland Bank which was founded in 1782 and local branches of both the Promstroi and MOST banks.

The big break came in 1990, when the reformed but Communist-led Latvian Government, keen to display its independence from Moscow, granted Parex a permit to deal in foreign currency. Kargins and the chairman of Parex, Victor Krasovitsky, opened the first currency exchange office in the USSR. This was a considerable achievement as they were allowed to deal in foreign currency, mainly conversion of the rouble into US dollars. The State had the monopoly in its insatiable quest for hard currency and any other

Homelike hospitality,
elegance and splendour
in the heart of Riga.

Your home in Riga

Comfort and homeliness...
a medieval whiff...

Hotel

dealings were illegal, and the offenders harshly prosecuted. At the time, the official rate was 60 kopeks to $1 but on the black market the value might have risen to 100 roubles to $1.

Parex developed quickly during perestroika and Latvia's independence, expanding outside its currency exchange operations to become a traditional bank, offering a range of services. Today, the bank is at the top of the official Latvian bank ratings and deals with about thirty per cent of the government's budget.

Victor Krasovitsky believes that the country is no longer a mere link with the East but is an entity in itself through its self-sufficiency policy. 'Latvia has always enjoyed good trading relations with the UK and up to World War II, the UK was its biggest trading partner,' he said. 'Our outlook has always been Western. Latvians have a Western mentality. A new class of business people have developed. They not only have a good education but are willing to devote their life to career building. We are fortunate, as many are employed in this bank.'

Entrepreneurs

Kargins estimates that there are some 100 millionaires in the country and that the BZs (in Latvia entrepreneurs are called the BZs from biezie which means thick wallets) will form a solid core for economic growth. You do not have to look far to see how crowded Riga is with BMWs and Mercedes that have smoked-glass windows. Inside the houses are large fridges, televisions and videos, which is a reminder what Budapest or Warsaw was like when the local entrepreneurs first got going.

Bank Success Story

Most entrepreneurs are thirtyish and one of the most successful stories concerned Girts Rungainis who built a bank from nothing to the sixth largest, within four years, and although capitalised at $11.8 million, its value rocketed to $40 million after a take-over. After graduating in Latvia, he went to Stockholm University to do a masters degree in banking and finance. There, to make ends meet, he cleaned windows.

On his return he founded the Deutsche-Lettish Bank. In 1995, he obtained the largest loan in the country from the European Bank of Reconstruction and Development and in 1996 achieved another record when his financial transaction was the biggest in Latvia with the sale of the bank to the Hansa Bank.

The business scene has changed dramatically since Independence when people could make a fortune overnight and lose it within a year, according to Girts Rungainis who has now set-up as an investment banker.

'We have good opportunities here', he said, elegantly clad in Yves St Laurent suit in his prestigious offices at 1 Dome Square, 'and excellent human resources as most people are well-educated. My only regret is that we have not yet been discovered by the key members of the European Union like the UK, Germany and France. We are only known by Northern Europe'.

(cont'd on page 28)

• TALE OF TWO MAYORS •

They stand like bookends at the beginning and end of the twentieth century, George Armitstead and Andris Berzins.

George Armitstead

Mayor from 1901-1912, he got the city off to a head start with a large exhibition to celebrate Riga's 700th year, in the Esplanade, a former parade ground which was turned later into a park. It was an excellent opportunity to demonstrate the city's diverse manufacturing products from ships, cars, railway carriages, motorcycles and bicycles to arts and crafts.

Armitstead came from an interesting background as his grandfather, who was also called George, emigrated from Yorkshire to seek his fortune in the flax business, which was booming in Latvia. He worked at an export company, Mitchel and Co. and later married a local rich girl, Emma von Jakobi. They had six children including John William, George's father.

The family was prominent in Riga. His uncle James was a chairman of the stock exchange and on his death bequeathed the city 500,000 roubles for building and maintaining the first hospital (which still exists today), as well as seventeen paintings from his art collection.

George was the eldest son and after graduating from Riga Polytechnic, the most advanced engineering institute in Russsia, he continued his studies at Zurich and Oxford Universities. In 1874, he married Cecily Pihlau and they had three daughters, one of whom was murdered by the Bolsheviks in 1919.

Before he was appointed Mayor, he was a successful businessman with interests in and outside the city. He founded the Volgunde Brickworks and was a director of both the Baltic Cellulose factory in Sloka and the Dinaburg-Vitebsk railway. In 1888, he chaired the committee of the fourth Baltic Agricultural Exhibition in Riga.

During his term as mayor, he changed the face of the city as most of the two-floor wooden houses were replaced by Art Nouveau buildings, and the Council prohibited the building of new wooden homes. As a result, they now comprise a third of all buildings in the town. The 700th anniversary provided the stimulus as no less than forty pavilions reflected this artisitic style. By the end of 1901 1,172 new projects were approved and it reached a peak in 1910 when approval was given for 1,359. In this area, he has left a lasting monument as the Art Nouveau architecture has been declared a World Heritage Site under UNESCO.

He encouraged the construction of public buildings such as nineteen schools and four hospitals and completed the National Theatre. Public gardens were also a priority and he had nine laid out throughout the city. His crowning achievement, is the creation of the first garden city, Kaiserwald (Tsar's forest now called Mezaparks), north of Riga city and bordering the Kisezers Lake shore.

Essentially there are three divisions in Mezaparks that include the large 1,037-acre (420-hectare) site in which the open-air auditorium is located and where the song festival with 20,000 singers and 40,000 members of the audience are accommodated. The Riga Zoo, which is one of the last projects Armitstead undertook, was opened in 1912 and occupies 59 acres (24 hectares). It is slightly south and just above the residential area, which is another architectural legacy of Armitstead.

The layout of the houses in the Forest Park (Mezaparks) was designed by Georg Kuphaldt, Director of Riga Parks and was begun at the same time as the middle of the city. Art Noveau, National Romanticism, Neo-Classicism and Rationalism are among the styles built in this former pine forest.

He is also credited with opening the first electric tram line (which is still in operation), the covered market and a bridge across the canal on Alexander Street. He was ranked by his contemporaries as the most successful mayor Riga ever had, and Tsar Nicholas II asked him to become Mayor of St Petersburg, a privilege that he declined.

He built himself a castle in the town of Tukums about 45 miles (72km) west of Riga, called Jaunmokas and it is one of the most outstanding examples of red brick style buildings in Latvia. His house can be found on 19 Marstalu Street and another belonging to the Armitstead family is on Nikolaja Street, Riga.

Andris Berzins

He is the mayor who has launched the 800th anniversary of the city initiative, Riga 800, which will be celebrated in 2001. He also has a British connection. He was born in a house in Anglikanu (English) Street opposite the English Seamen's Club (now the Danish Embassy).

The key elements of Riga 800 are humanisation of the city environment through improving transport, building a new bridge across the Daugava, and the creation of a recreation zone. The plan is ambitious as it encompasses the improvement of drinking water and clean air and development of tourism and service industries.

Andris Berzins is a historian and often trips up Swedish visitors with the question 'Which was the biggest city in Sweden during the sixteenth century?' The correct answer is Riga – not Stockholm' as Latvia was part of Sweden at the time. He reminds visitors that Riga of the Thirties was one of the cleanest and most elegant cities in Europe and called Paris of the North or Little Paris.

Although a third of the country's population lives in the city, he manages with only a budget of $340,000,000 a year.

Andris Berzins

Skarnu Street with St George's Church
(now part of the Museum of Decorative
and Applied Art) in the foreground and
St John's Church in the background

LATVIA'S *Finest*
Since 1865
BREWING
Traditions

Aldaris

ZELTA

Another remarkable entrepreneur, who is already using western marketing methods – an unusual feature in the business world, to grow his television company is Andrejs Ekis. He is full of Murdoch quotes such as 'Think global, be local' and I am sure if the media tycoon came to hear of him, he would snap him up and get him to establish an empire in Russia and Eastern Europe. 'I started with an idea to create breakfast television' he said, 'and then I bought a company that transmitted the evening news. Next I filled the space in between and had the first and only independent TV station in the country'.

Again only thirtyish, he is now the biggest player in the market and reaches eighty-six per cent of the Latvian population. He appreciates that Riga is a cosmopolitan city,

• BEERS •

Move over Prague and Munich there will soon be another beer capital on the scene. When the rest of Europe discovers Latvian beer, Riga will be put on the map as the place to visit for a fest of real ale.

There are unknown and exotic tastes and aromas to be sampled over a wide range of brands, bottled, on tap and from micro breweries. The beers of great quality are produced by craftsmen and deserve the same consideration as that given to wine. Many visitors in fact rave about these products and drink them instead of wine with their meals. Pale summer ales predominate because most of the beer is drunk during the midsummer festival of Ligo.

The most popular brewery, **Aldaris**, sets the pace because its quality standards are comparable to or even exceed the best in Europe and it still maintains the traditional brewing methods from 1865, when it was established.

An unusual feature of the brewery is that the master brewer is a woman, Inara Sure. She ensures that only natural ingredients are used and recommends connoisseurs to drink Luxus with fish and Zelta with meat. I prefer the Porteris myself, a dark beer which has a high alcohol content of seven per cent. It has a caramel taste with an aroma of wine.

The beer with the most unique taste originates from one of the oldest breweries in the country. Four hundred years old, the Cesis Castle is located in the village of Cesis where the largest beer festival is held every year.

Stalin's preferred beer, Rigas Originalis is pale but with a depth of bitterness that clings to the palate. For those who like lager, (gaisais in Latvian), Bauska is your brand and it is produced by the oldest brewery, so old that there is a folk song about the beer. Other brands worth mentioning include Piebalgas, Tervetes, Dzintars Karla and another strong dark beer, Satans.

Micro breweries are found in every region and the Brenguli is located in a town of the same name about three and a half miles (6km) east of Valmeira. The brewery has its fans who like the bitter which is unfiltered or processed and is described simply as having, 'rich malt aroma and a bitter hop edge'.

the largest in northern Europe and although the country, with its 2.5 million population, is small there are terrific opportunities, particularly if one uses the country as a stepping-stone to the vast Russian market.

'We have all the facilities in this country to launch products into the CIS' he said. 'We can use

Language

Riga is a cosmopolitan city and although Latvian is the official language, English, Russian and German are widely spoken. Latvian is an Indo-European language, which belongs to the Balt group like Lithuanian, and has been spoken for a period of 4,000 years. It is closely related to Sanskrit and an interesting link between them for example is the word for water, *ava*, that is synonymous with *Daugava*, Latvian for river. For interest it should be noted that all male names end in 's' and female names either 'a' or 'e'.

top Russian actors and have a measure of their psychology. The biggest mistake westerners make is to deal directly with them. The Russians consider a western businessman as a duck they can hunt. There are countless stories of how money disappears and no one knows where'. He admits that there are problems with bureaucracy but points out that you can always find a reasonable official.

Food, cuisine and drink

There is a world of difference between food and cuisine and both are obtainable in Riga. The food is similar to other northern European destinations, heavy and solid, which is well suited to the climate.

Latvian specialties

However, there are surprises in their specialties, soups galore for both summer and winter: beetroot or borsch and sour cream barley soup (skaba putra) served cold for hot weather; for below zero temperatures there is cabbage soup or dried pea and bacon soup which is so thick that it can be described as a stew and is considered to be a national dish. Another unusual soup is a milk fish soup called zivjupiena.

Main courses include simply adding meatballs to the soups, pork in aspic which has accompaniments of mustard or horseradish, potato pancakes served with sour cream and a wide range of smoked meat and fish, particularly sprats for which the region is famous. Piragi, a pastry filled with bacon or other meat and onions is popular and no celebration is complete without it.

Desserts recommended are the Alexander torte, raspberry or cranberry filled pastry strips and a bread pudding or Rupjmaizins pudins made with black or rye bread which is as light and tasty as any French patisserie.

The Central Market

For a quick introduction to Latvian food you can do no better than go to the Central Market next to the Railway Station. Les Halles and Covent Garden have disappeared and it is refreshing to find this remarkable landmark still intact. 'It's a unique experience to visit these vast halls that housed airships', said Oliver Staas, General Manager at Radisson SAS Hotel. 'The buildings are still in good condition. I go once a week with my chef as the quality of food is outstanding.' Each Zeppelin hangar exclusively sells either meat, fish, dairy products or fruit and vegetables. The market is open daily from 8am to 5pm. On Sundays it closes at 3pm.

Top restaurateurs

With cuisine the territory in Riga is divided into two areas, Vincents and Zagars; the celebrity chef versus the latter-day Conran. If you come to Latvia you have to try either one or both.

Martins Ritins

Martins Ritins, who runs Vincents in its various forms from official event catering, the restaurant, and teaching students to the celebrity chef weekly television show, is British, born of Latvian parents who left during the last war. He returned to the country in 1992 after working as a cook in Canada, Saudi Arabia and Jamaica. There were no private restaurants at the time and he opened the first, Vincents, which is named after the famous artist. 'When I arrived there were only canteens to eat in', he said. 'Institutionalised cooking in fact reigned supreme'.

He recalled that when he introduced leaf salads to his menus, many customers sent the food back to the kitchen. Their message was, 'This is food for rabbits, where's the potatoes and meat?'

The food scene is slowly changing and Rigans are coming round to healthier eating. He is a pioneer and besides influencing people's palates, he is encouraging farmers to grow healthier grains or breed quality stock. An inveterate foodie, he raves about a bottle of aromatic extra virgin olive oil and the wild mushrooms he can buy for only £1.50 a kilo rather than £40 a kilo in the UK.

His appreciative clients include ambassadors and celebrities like B B King, Rostropovitch, José Carreras and the British Royal family. Both Prince Charles and Prince Andrew came to dine. During the summer if you sit on the terrace you can enjoy Charolais beef steak, guinea fowl or sushi and watch the in-crowd of the city.

Andrejs Zagars

Andrejs Zagars, is a restaurant owner of the same ilk as Terence Conran and is known as a trend-setter. An actor by profession, he decided to travel during the 1980s when restrictions were removed and turn his artistic flair to creating a new cuisine in a designer environment. Customers would be attracted by the ambience, the visual presentation of the food, its quality, the service and innovative menu.

'The client doesn't just pay for a piece of meat but for the combined bouquet', he said. 'My new establishment called The New Zagars Restaurant, has trendy, fusion crossover food, a Californian kitchen'.

But the three restaurants are not the only places he has in the city. There is a wine shop, Symposium Vini, as well as a bar, Deco next door to the Symposium Restaurant in Berga Bazaars. The Osiris coffee bar is also one of three in-places to go. There would be no difficulty for the trendy foodies in London, New York, or other US cities to feel at home in his places. He plans to open a Latvian restaurant unpolluted by German Kitsch. 'The traditional food is heavy and fatty but can be made more interesting and healthy', he said.

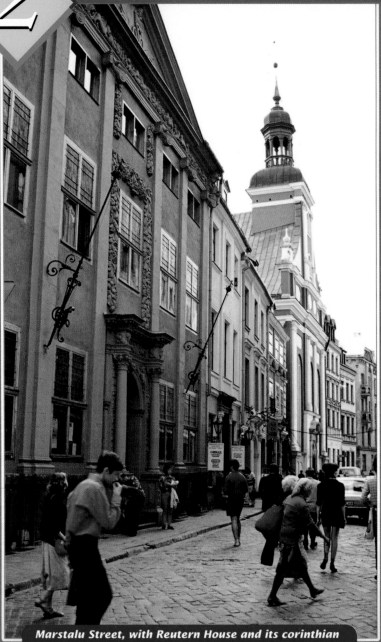

Marstalu Street, with Reutern House and its corinthian columned entrance in foreground and tower of Reformed Church in the background

Walking is one of the best ways to get the feel of a city and Riga is no exception. Two walks are described here, the first exploring Vecriga and the second looking at the wonderful Art Nouveau architecture to be found here.

TOUR ONE: OLD RIGA OR VECRIGA

The tour begins at the **Gunpowder Tower**, a striking red brick building with dolomite foundations, which is located at the intersection of **Smilsu** and **Torna Streets**. The tower, which was built at the beginning of the fourteenth century is part of the medieval wall. It is

KEY

① Jacob's Barracks – Remains of the 16th-19th C Defensive Wall
② Medieval (15th C) Wall (Remains of the 13th-15th C Def. Syst.)
③ Swedish Gate & Troksnu Street
④ Parliament House
⑤ St Jacob's Church
⑥ 'Three Brothers' Medieval/17th C Houses
⑦ Riga Castle
⑧ Anglican Church

⑨ English Club (now Danish Embassy)
⑩ Dome Cathedral
⑪ Blackhead's House & former Town Square
⑫ St Peter's Church
⑬ Mentzendorf's House – Museum (16th-19th C)
⑭ Dannenstern's House – Museum (17th-19th C)
⑮ Armitstead's House
⑯ Traditional 17th C Warehouses of Riga
⑰ Reitern's House (now House of Journalists)
⑱ St John's Church
⑲ Convent Enclosure
⑳ The Small or Craftsmen Guild (altered in 19th C)
㉑ The Large or Tradesmen Guild (altered in 19th C)

the only one of the twenty-five towers left and was in use until the sixteenth century. The distance between each tower was determined by the range of an arrow, which was around 22ft (7m).

It acquired its name during the Swedish period when gunpowder was stored there and to ensure durability, three horse heads have been immured in the 1ft (31cm) thick tower walls.

Another name for the building was Smilsu or Sand tower because the city was surrounded by sand hills and the tower also served as a main entrance to the city because a gatehouse was placed next to it. Relics of earlier periods can be seen including rings for securing cannons in the windows, the thick walls that could withstand the impact of cannon balls (nine Russian balls are embedded in the walls) and a vaulted chamber which was the assembly point for the soldiers. (This is where the café is now located). There are good views from the tower of the old town.

The **Latvian War Museum** is housed in the tower and is devoted to military history, particularly featuring exhibits that depict the country's struggle for independence. Of special interest is the Latvian Riflemen or Strelnieks, both white and red, whose exploits were so remarkable that they served as Lenin's special guards in the Kremlin.

Walk down Torna Street and on the right is **Jacob's Barracks**, which runs the whole length of the street. The building with basements is the longest in the city and was built in the eighteenth century. On the left are the restored remnants of the city wall (thirteenth to fifteenth century) which included the small rectangular Ramer's tower.

Further along are several private houses and at Number Eleven you will find the **Swedish Gate** which was built in 1698 when Riga was part of Sweden and its largest city. It was one of the eight gates of the defending wall and was opened at sunrise and closed at sunset. Inside the building, which is now the **House of Latvian Architects**, extending from the basement to the first floor are the remains of another tower, the Jirgens.

Ghostly cries

Again there is a tale of an immurement or rather two tales. A Latvian girl fell in love with a Swedish soldier and wanted to marry him. Such a relationship was forbidden and she was caught and entombed alive in the wall. Another variation also concerns a young girl who tried to escape the city during the black plague but was caught and given the same treatment. Whichever story is true, her cries can be heard on New Year's Eve.

It is traditional for newly weds to walk through the Swedish Gate to ensure a happy life. The house was the first to be owned privately in the city and was bought in 1679 by Ivan Serpentin. Two rooms in the house are open to the public.

Walk through the Swedish Gate and turn right into Troksnu or Alarm Street. This is a vestige of the inner side of the defending wall, where townsmen had to congregate to defend the city against attackers. Notice the uneven cobbles which resulted from a regulation that required the citizens to maintain the street by supplying cobble stones. Each craft had to be responsible for a sector and had to equip their members with armaments and six leather buckets.

At the end of the street you will face **The Saeima or Parliament Building**, which was originally, the Vidzeme Knight's House or House of the Nobles. It was reconstructed in 1867 in the style of a Florentine Renaissance Palace by prominent Latvian architects Janis F Baumanis and Robert Pflug. After the Agrarian reforms in 1920, it became the Latvian parliament.

Turn left in Jacob Street and follow the building round into Klostera or Monastery Street. There you will find one of the three important landmarks of the city which appeared on medieval maps and provided the famous view: St Jacob's Cathedral. The cathedral was build in 1225 for people in the suburbs and the poor to worship as it was then located outside the city wall, (the rich had the Dome) and is the only church which still has a Gothic spire. It has a unique feature on the southern side, a bell that hung under a protective cupola outside the spire. If you look up you will still be able to see the cupola as the 'balcony bell' has long since been removed.

The bell was also called the 'wretched sinner's bell' as one of the uses was to announce that a hanging would take place in the Town Hall square. (The last hangman, incidentally, lived at 9 Torna Street and the occupation was hereditary). Another meaning

associated with the bell was that it would automatically ring whenever an unfaithful wife passed below. There was a period when it rang continually and this so upset the townspeople that it was taken down and thrown into the Daugava. The bell has never been replaced.

Changes of allegiance

The cathedral has a mixed religious history. First it was for Catholics and during the Reformation its status changed and it became the first church to hold a Lutheran service in 1522. When the Polish King Stepan Bathory conquered the city in 1582, it was handed over to the Jesuits. In 1621, when the Swedes arrived, St Jacobs became a garrison church. For the next three centuries it remained in the Protestant camp until the twentieth century when it reverted to Catholicism.

As a cathedral it has a rather austere basilica interior and as you enter, inscribed on the portal is *Misericordias domini in aeternum cantabo*, translated as 'Sing the Lord's mercy forever'. It is white inside with brickwork that outlines the different shapes such as the vaulted ceiling, arches and windows. The altar is simple and the cathedral has a choir room, a parish hall and a 27ft (8m) tall steeple.

There is evidence of two entombments in the cathedral. In the northern wall a niche was found to contain a man's skeleton

Top Ten Architectural Styles

A list of the top ten buildings in Riga which should not be missed by anyone with an interest in architecture, has been compiled with the co-operation of Irena Bakule of the Latvian State Inspection for Heritage Protection.

1. Art Nouveau buildings in The Old Town, the following streets have three or more buildings: Kalku, Smilsu, Marstalu, Skunu, Valnu and Alberta Street.
2. St Peter's Church with viewing platform.
3. Dome Cathedral and its organ.
4. Mentzendorff House Museum corner of Grecinieku and Kungu Streets (opposite).
5. Reutern House, 2 Marstalu Street.
6. Kemeri Hotel, Kemeri and Hotel Majori, Majori (see page 67).
7. St Saviours Anglican Church in Anglikanu Street.
8. Ethnographic Open-air Museum, 440 Brivibas Street, just outside city limits.
9. Jacob's barracks in Torna Street.
10. Konventa Seta complex between Kaleju and Skarnu Streets which includes oldest building, St George's Church.

with his clothes which were well preserved and showed that the person was from the upper classes. The other entombment was of a man called Indrikis and is described in documents at the city archives. He wanted to be worshipped in this life and the next and therefore wanted to be buried alive in the walls. The Brothers of the Franciscan monastery who had jurisdiction of the cathedral agreed to his request.

The building is an amalgam of different periods. The main part dates back to the thirteenth century, the cupola for the outside bell was added during the fifteenth century, the lower part of the octagonal tower two centuries later and its roof pyramid in 1756.

Opposite the cathedral is the eighteenth-century **church of Mary Magdalene** that was also once a convent. Walk down the street towards Maza Pils or Small Castle Street which when you turn right leads to Riga Castle.

Facing you are **'The Three Brothers'** at No.'s 17, 19 and 21, which are outstanding medieval architectural monuments. The nickname derives from the fact that they represent residential buildings from the fifteenth, sixteenth and seventeenth century respectively which are adjacent. Each house has a gable, the simplest design is

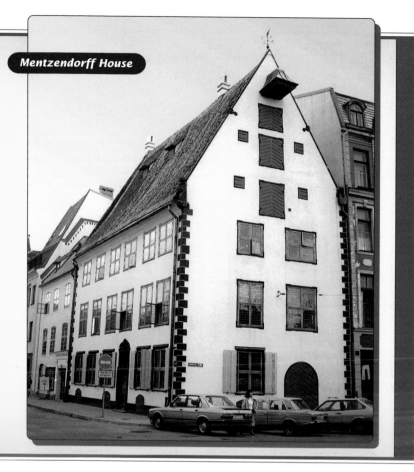

No.17, which ascends in three steps with Gothic niches, slightly askew and is the oldest stone house in the city.

It is also the furthest from the street as the space in front was used as a porch for benches and beside the door are two large identity stones. A clue to the former owner is given by the coat of arms that includes ears of wheat. It belonged to a baker and was the site of the first pastry shop. The other two are closer to the street as space was at a premium and additional floors were added.

The **Museum of Architecture** is housed in No.19 and it is worth a visit to get an impression of the inside of this sixteenth-century building. Examples of models, plans and sketches of Johann Felsko, Janis Baumanis and others can also be seen. The building, which was renovated in 1646, has an interior also from the same period including a fireplace.

All the Brothers had similar interior layouts as the ground and first floors were used for living space for the family and servants, while the upper floors including the attic, were used for storage. Hatches were placed in the middle of the ceiling to move goods up and down on a system of pulleys. Sometimes access was also gained by placing beams outside the building for lifting big and heavy objects into attic storage rooms.

Riga Castle is found at the end of the street which becomes the Castle Square or Pils Laukums. The present castle building, originally square-shaped with four towers including two rounded ones, was built in 1515 by the townsmen. They had already destroyed three earlier buildings of the Brothers of the Sword and the Livonian Order who decided it was safer to be outside the city walls.

Hated citizen

The last Grand Master of the Livonian Order, Walter von Plettenberg, added his sculptural relief to the patroness of the Order, St Mary and both were placed above the gate. He was held in such odium by citizens that he eventually left Riga and spent his last years in Cesis.

During the Swedish and Russian periods an additional wing was added on the northern side including a polygonal bay window tower which had limestone carvings of animals, men and gargoyles. The reliefs, splendid examples of seventeenth-century decorative art, can be seen if you walk round it. A fifth tower, designed by Eizens Laube, the three-star tower of national unity was added in 1938.

The castle is the residence of the President of Latvia, Vaira Vike-Freiberga, and also contains magnificent reception halls. She has her own orchestra, the Latvian army band which plays on ceremonial occasions. Whenever she is at home, the special Presidential flag flies from the Holy Ghost Tower which served as part of the city's fortifications and is opposite the Lead Tower with its conical roof. The Castle also houses three museums, the **Museum of Foreign Art**, the **Museum of Latvian History** and the **Rainis Museum of Literature and Art**.

As you leave the Castle head for the river down **Daugava Gate**. Turn left into the **11th November Embankment** which, was the site of the Daugavmala or Daugava's edge market for almost four centuries, and again take the second left into Anglikanu or Anglican Street. This is named after the **Factory Church of St Saviour of Riga** and was built by British merchants in 1859.

Over two thousand English ships visited Riga every year during the eighteenth century and religious services were shared with German and Dutch sailors and merchants in the Reformation Church in Marstalu Street. The arrangement was unsatisfactory as they were conducted in German.

Another bit of Britain was built at the end of the street, a club for English Officers, some forty years

English Church

Representatives of the English Trading Company gained permission from the Tsar to erect their own church. The Neo-Gothic building, a classic example of the Eclectic style was designed by Johann Daniel Felsko and was built on English soil which was part of the foundation. The bricks too later. As you pass you can notice three reliefs above the window of the balcony, a shamrock, a rose and a thistle. Each are symbols for Ireland, England and Scotland respectively.

The club, now the **Danish Embassy**, was designed by the well-known Latvian architect Wilhelm Bockslaff who also has several other fine buildings to his credit including Art Nouveau style at 25 Jauniela and 6 Kalku Streets, Armitstead's Jaunmokas Castle and the red brick Latvian Academy of Art. The richest merchants in Riga were the British whose influence lasted until World War II. During the 1890s, half the export trade of Latvia was with the UK.

We now turn right into Pils or Castle Street and head for the heart of Old Riga, the **Dome Square. The Dome**, which originates from Domus Dei (The House of God) was the seat of Bishop Albert and one of the three powers in the city sharing influence with the Town Hall and Livonian Order. Bishop Albert consecrated an ancient burial ground of the original inhabitants, the Curonians or the Cours, in 1211 and started to build the

came from England and were brought as ballast in ships. The cost of the project came to some 86,000 roubles. The Church was conveniently situated near the river and enabled English ships to dock not far away so that the sailors and merchants could attend services before going about their business.

church which would later become the largest in The Baltics. It is a superb artistic and architectural landmark and has dominated the city's skyline for almost seven centuries.

At a lower elevation than other buildings it was a victim of floods during 1709 and an embankment was built on Jauniela Street to prevent inundation in the future. The original foundation marks the original level of Riga and shows how the debris was built up over the centuries, giving the wrong impression that subsidence has occurred. The thirteenth-century Gothic portal, formerly the main entrance, appears now to be buried. To gain entry to the northern portal one has to descend sixteen steps. It was built on the cross but this has been obscured through multiple additions during various periods.

The church's oldest sections, the altar alcove and east wing crossing, are excellent examples of the early Romanesque-style with its high walls, rows of semi-circular windows and crosswise vaulted ceiling. The Gothic style extensions are distinguished by their simplicity – pointed arches, stellar vaults and large windows. The eastern pediment and the steeple were reconstructed in 1776 in the Baroque manner.

The portal was refashioned by Johann Felsko in 1862 and the new Art Nouveau vestibule was completed at the turn of the last century. Although the architectural features inside highlight its grandeur, the highly decorative interiors were lost during the Reformation and what was left was mostly removed

(cont'd on page 43)

Enter the church from the western portal and turn left into St Mary's Chapel. The old altar was once installed here and because it was low the view of the new stained glass windows was not obscured but it disappeared when concerts were held.

We move towards the northern side and the Tiesenhausen Chapel which was dedicated to one of the oldest families in the Baltic states. The Tiesenhausens donated two stained glass windows in 1883, one of which depicts the family with the Virgin Mary and angels and the other is of Bishop Albert with the builder of the Dome. The epitaph and grave plaque of an earlier ancestor, Mary Tiesenhausen, who died in 1611, is attached to the wall.

There are two further stained glass windows in the next chapel which show historical events of 1525 and 1621 respectively. The Grand Master of the Livonian Order, Walter von Plettenberg, read his edict on religious freedom in the Town Square and vowed to protect the citizens from the Catholic Archbishop's claim to restore Catholicism. The Swedish King, Gustavus Adolfus, in his moment of triumph was welcomed by the Mayor of Riga, Herman Samson and the Town Councillors in front of the Dome after he had conquered the city. They were pleased with the King as he had liberated them from the yoke of Catholic Poland.

Below: Interior, 13th and 15th century with grave plaques on the wall
Opposite: Aerial view of the Dome and Dome Square

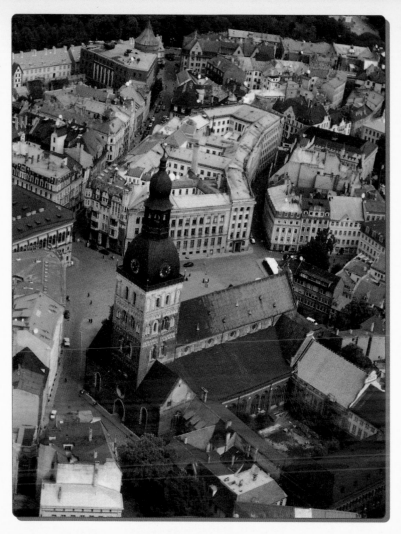

At the northern wing crossing, there are stained glass side windows designed by the local artist Ernst Tode in 1902 who also provided the Art Nouveau-style stained glass windows at the Latvian Academy of Art. Two windows describe the lives of St Martin and St George, while the third, which was made in the Urbana workshops in Dresden, depict the Apostles Peter and Paul.

There is a memorial at the crossing, of the notorious mayor Nicolas Ecke, who appears to have embezzled funds while he was the city's treasurer. He was so reviled by the citizens that he was thrown out of the city on two occasions. Before his

(cont'd oveleaf)

(cont'd from previous page)

death however, he tried to make amends through the establishment of a home for six or more old, poor widows at 22 Skarnu Street, the Ecke's Convent. To assuage their fury, he had inscribed on the façade, the words, 'The aim of my life is Christ', which was placed above a relief of Christ and The Sinner, implying, 'Let him who is without sin throw the first stone'. All this was to no avail as an alabaster head of him, which adorned the memorial, was broken off. It was replaced in the last century.

At the altar niche are three stained glass windows which were made at the Weber and Kalerta workshops, with an image of Christ in the middle, a scene from the Old Testament on the left and on the right one from the New Testament. Along the wall is an exciting find, two long benches, which date from pre-Reformation days, with fine carvings on both. There is a picture of Adam and Eve in the Garden of Eden on one and of Mary Magdalene on the other.

The only grave in the Dome is found here in the left wall. It is of Bishop Meinhard who built the first stone and brick church at Ikskile, south of Riga on the Daugava River. He died in 1196 and his remains were brought to the Dome for burial in the fourteenth century.

At the crossing of the south wing, we find further stained glass windows depicting scenes from both the Old and New Testament. On the wall is a plaque denoting the water level during the 1709 flood.

In the central area we can see the magnificent organ and the memorable pulpit which both feature fine woodwork. The pulpit, which was gifted to the church in 1641, was supposedly designed and carved by Tobias Heinz, the artist from Jelgava, and the angel was sculptured by Imhof in 1817. The pews, ornamented with black heads, are for the Society's members *(see Blackhead's House)*.

The organ, which has always been considered as the Dome's greatest treasure, has 6718 pipes with 124 pitches, two consoles with four manuals and a pediclavier. When it was completed and installed in 1884 by Walcker Ludvigsburg, it was the largest in the world.

The original organ was designed by Jakob Raabs in 1601 in the Mannerism style and embellished with Baroque and Rococo motifs in the seventeenth and eighteenth century. The woodwork was decorated with fantastic animals, angels and wreaths of flowers.

during Soviet times when the church was converted into a concert hall in 1960.

Outside in the huge Dome square you can comprend why everyone usually ends up there as seven streets converge on the square and cafés as well as street markets are popular in the area.

Weather vanes

On the south side the golden cock can be seen and the windows which sported stained glass that were destroyed during the war are bricked in. The original weathercock was two-sided, a gold and a black side. When ships saw the black cock, it represented bad weather and there would be no entry into the port. Before you head towards Kramu or Garbage Street go to the middle of the square and you can see the three golden weather cocks on St Peter's, the Dome and St Jacob's.

Pass along Kramu Street, across Kalku and veer right where you will find the former Town Hall Square and the most splendid building in the city. There, the **Blackheads' House**, or Melngalvju, was a society of unmarried, rich foreign merchants that originated in the thirteenth century, initially under the patronage of St Mauritius. He was a black martyr who had been a tribune in a Roman Legion and the coat of arms consisted of an oval gold frame surrounding a black turbaned head, a sword and a cross against a red background.

Later there were other patrons including St George and St Gertrude.

The building, which is being restored, was first mentioned in 1334 when it housed part of the Riga Guild, and it was only later in 1477 that it became associated with the Blackheads, through their rental of the upper floors. They acquired the building in 1713.

A unique feature of the house is the vast ornate gable which was derived from Dutch influences. Adrian and Lambert Jensen supervised the rich ornamentation that included crowning the stepped gable with sculptures of people such as St George and St Gertrude, animals and obelisks. The steps of the gable were decorated with intertwined ribbons, and spirals carved in stone. The six inches (15cm) of the pediment had paintings of deities like Mercury and Neptune, and a tower clock with an 'eternal clock calendar' showing the month, day, hour, minute and phase of the moon, was placed above the central niches in 1622. A relief bust of King Arthur too was included in a shallow niche, as both the King and his Knights of the Round Table were an integral part of their social activities.

The top of the gable was crowned by a remarkable feature, three metallic poles. The central pole, which was the longest and made of gilded copper, carried the remarkable weathercock representing St George and the Dragon, with a sword in his hand. It weighed some 66lbs (30 kg) and was made by the Riga jewel maker Eberhard Meyer in 1622.

Through its regulations, the society resembles a British Club and *(cont'd on page 46)*

'Riga
*– the hottest
city in the north'*

For future information:
Riga Dome City Council, Valdemara iela 3, Riga LV-1539, Latvia
Phone: +371 702 6177. Fax: +371 702 6337

one would imagine that women, married or otherwise, would have been barred as no married men could be members. Card and dice games were prohibited as well as carrying swords into the premises. There was no doubt as to who was welcome there as there was a stricture that did not allow soldiers or craftsmen entry, as it was for officers only, starting with ensigns. The members actively participated in social life, founded schools and established charities. They had balls at which women were welcome, as on an occasion in 1762 when Catherine II arrived incognito and joined in the dancing.

Opposite the Blackheads, is **St Peter's Church** which has always been a familiar landmark because it was the tallest building in the city. It has always been the stronghold of the citizens and Town Council and was the base of their power in the city. Built in the thirteenth century, it was mentioned in a chronicle in 1297 when citizens bombarded the castle with stones from its tower during clashes with the Livonian Order of Knights.

Some believe that the church is the most beautiful in Riga because of the symmetrical shape and the spire which is a masterpiece of fusion of Gothic and Baroque styles. But the spire has had its share of bad luck with several fires and when it was struck by lightening Peter the Great was on hand and helped to prevent the fire from spreading to nearby houses. (The Tsar lived in the city for a period and his castle is found at 9 Palace Street). The last spire fortunately lasted the longest from 1746 to 1940, some 195 years. Sadly little has survived from its past glory when the church was burnt down in 1941 and rebuilt in 1984.

There are two viewing platforms in the belfry which enable visitors to see the panorama of the city as well as the sea on a clear day. We leave the church and move in the direction of The Blackheads House before turning left towards the corner of Grecinieku or Sinners and Kungu or Masters' Streets where the wealthy merchant Mentzendorff's house is located *(see page 48)*.

The seventeenth century was a prosperous period for Riga because of the great demand in western Europe for timber, flax, hemp and grain from the East. Riga served as the point of transhipment at a time when Russia had no access to the Baltic and the trade enriched merchants in the city.

For a glimpse of the sort of people involved look no further than a painting by an unknown artist which hangs in the **Museum of the History of Riga and Navigation**. A group of men in dark garments with broad collars sit on high chairs round a table covered with black cloth. Each person has a pile of money in front of him and they share a large silver mug of beer and a goblet of wine. Such profitable trade stimulated shipbuilding as well as the construction of magnificent many floored houses with attics on four to five floors for storage *(see page 36)*.

Once in Kungu Street note the cupola at the top of the house on the Grecinieku side where pulleys would be operated. Cupolas are found in most medieval houses. Walk down Kungu and turn first right into Peldu or Swim Street in the direction of the Daugava and turn left into the 11th November Embankment and left again into Marstalu Street.

Dannenstern House at No.21 is an excellent example of Baroque architecture with an unusual feature of glazed roof tiles. It was owned by Ernst Metsue, a self-made man of Dutch origin who started off as a tradesman and ended up with a fleet of vessels. He was rich enough to build, in 1696, the largest private house in Riga. On the way up he acquired the title of von Dannenstern. The façade is decorated with eight pilasters crowned with elegant capitals. Stone heads of fantastic animals are on the right and left side of the roof and the two entrances are richly decorated with stone carvings. A Swedish sculptor, D Walter and a Swiss stonemason created the magnificent façade.

A large hall, an office and the business quarters were on the ground floor. The family rooms are spread over two floors, the first and the second. The vast attic was used as a storeroom and goods were also stored in the basements.

Marstalu or Mary's Stable Street is worth lingering in, as there are several other interesting buildings. Next door at No.19 is where George Armitstead, a former mayor, lived *(see entry, Tale of Two Mayors)*. Move up the street towards Audeja or Weaver Street. On the right, you can spot a steeple that will indicate the **Reformed Church**, at the corner of Alksnaja or Alder Grove Street, and one of the few Calvinist places of worship.

The church was built by Kristofers Meinert, who was the grandfather of the famous Latvian architect Kristofers Haberland. The latter was responsible for many houses in Riga in the Classical style which had the singular features of façades decorated with columns on either side of the door and a central window with balcony above on the first floor. They were built of bricks with flat ceilings and only basements were vaulted *(see No.5 Smilsu Street)*. It is the only Baroque church in the city and in a break with tradition, has a star rather than a cock as a weathervane. The upper part of the façade is crowned with a cupola and open gallery, a design more common in northern Europe than the Baltics.

When it was rebuilt after a fire in 1805, the first floor was lifted and storerooms created under it. These spaces have now been turned into a concert hall and restaurant respectively.

We will first go down **Alksnaja** to see a traditional seventeenth-century warehouse before returning to the top of Marstalu Street. As trade boomed, the attic storerooms became insufficient and purpose-built storehouses were constructed. They were large brick or stone buildings with tiled roofs and their butt-ends faced the street, such as No's.7, 8, 10 and 11 which remains entirely unchanged.

The roof rested on a row of strong beams that ran the width of the building. The doors were usually made of oakwood and a stone emblem, representing a bird, animal or strange beast was placed above the door or next to it. Sometimes the animal would be simply painted on a wall.

(cont'd on page 50)

Wealthy Merchants' houses

Mentzendorff's House and **Dannenstern's House** are excellent examples of the above. The former was built in 1695 by Jurgen Helm, a Town Councillor, and was bought in 1884 by the wealthy merchant August Mentzendorff whose descendants lived here until the last war.

For over 200 years it has had a dual use as a family home and a pharmacy owned by the Briedis's. A fascinating interior belies the plain, austere exterior and the museum, an affiliate of the Museum of History of Riga and Navigation, is worth a visit. It has been furnished and decorated with authentic pieces from the seventeenth and eighteenth centuries, and gives the visitor a good impression of life during those periods.

On the ground floor, there is an open fireplace with copper and tin kitchen utensils and the laboratory and shop, with a rare cash collegiate desk. Each floor surprises: there is a Watteau room where the walls are painted with motifs from Antoine Watteau works; a small family chapel; a Bohemian room of a young poet; a living room with an old piano, old masters on the wall and a card-desk with an ancient deck of cards; and the big entrance hall with the clay floor.

There is an interesting display of products in the chemist shop including Riga's Black Balsam. Its healing qualities were attributed mainly to its application to wounds, stings, tumours and fractured bones. Little thought was given to quaffing it. The museum is open 10am to 5pm, Wednesday to Sunday, ☎ 721 2951 and ☎ 722 2636.

Open 17th century fireplace in Mentzendorff's House

A view over St Peter's Church towards the canal and parks of the new city. At the top left, the red Gunpowder tower with its conical roof

Identity and superstition

A stone camel can be seen above the door on Valnu Street at the Big Camel. This had a dual purpose as warehouses did not have numbers and could easily be identified as the elephant or dove which can be seen on the façade of Sport's Museum No.7. The other reason was superstition, as the Rigans believed such emblems would ward off the evil spirits and protect their merchandise.

Under the roof of the warehouse in the courtyard was a special device for lifting goods. It was a windlass fastened to a beam and men would pull the rope tied to the goods up or down to the desired floor. In some instances there was a tower with a spiral staircase that led up to the windlass such as No.11.

During the eighteenth century there were about 160 warehouses in the city and some ten can still be found on Vecpilsetas Street. If you wish to see the inside of an old warehouse, the one at 3 Vecpilsetas has been transformed into a restaurant called The Big Camel.

We move round the corner to the beginning of Marstalu Street where we find another seventeenth-century building, **Reutern House**, that belonged to John Reutern, another Dutch merchant of the same name. It was designed by Rupert Bindenschuh, who set a trend by abandoning the gabled style and adopting Baroque. Instead he used Corinthian columns and portraits of the owners of the house above them. The façade is also decorated with a group of sculptures depicting a battle between a bear and lion that represented the Northern War at the beginning of the eighteenth century between Sweden and Russia.

Of particular beauty are the stone garlands over the first floor windows and running along the upper part of the building, above the six pilasters, is a stone frieze representing animals alternating with leaves and flowers. The splendid façade has been preserved for over three centuries while the interior was refurbished several times. It is now the Journalists' House.

Reutern family anecdotes

Reutern was so pleased with his house after completion that he gave the architect a silver goblet in appreciation. He was also fined for driving around in a carriage with glass windows, which at the time was considered the height of immorality.

One of the members of the Reutern family, Gerhard Wilhelm, who was a painter and engraver was also a friend of Goethe. He was at the Russian court during the Napoleonic War and served as an adjutant of General Barclay de Tolley. Wounded during a battle he could afterwards only paint with his left hand. Later, he founded the first artists' colony in Germany at Willingshausen in Hessen.

We are now off to see the fourth and last church and head left towards Skarnu or Butcher's Street, which was the site of the former meat market. There is a connection between **St John's Church** and Reutern House as the architect, Rupert Bindershuh, who died in 1698, is buried there.

The church and a cloister was built by the Dominican friars in the thirteenth century when Bishop Nicholas gave them the former Bishop's palace, which was built by Bishop Albert. In 1500 the church was rebuilt after a fire and except for the monastery gates and north-west entrance everything was new. A high-stepped pediment was built above the north-west wall, its vertical stripes of red brick alternate with lightly-hued plaster work.

Sinful monks

Two monks' heads with their mouths open are mounted high on the south-west wall and below them is an opening in the wall, covered with a grating. They are symbols of the vain ambition of a couple of Dominicans who wanted to ward off evil on St John's Church and decided to become immured. For a time they lived inside the wall, being fed by passers-by. When they died the Pope did not declare them saints because the church did not benefit from their deaths and pronounced their actions sinful.

Life-size, sandstone statues of John the Baptist in prison and Salome carrying his head are installed in niches on the wall in Jana or John Street, where the first Riga castle occupied by Bishop Albert was situated. Distinctive features inside are the net vaults, its Baroque altar, the August Stilling altar pieces and stained glass windows. The painting by Janis Rozentals called *The Crucified* is in the Sacristy *(see page 99)*.

We now enter Jana Seta or John's courtyard, a narrow passage between the church and Ecke's Convent. The cloister gate with its Gothic frame, has embellishment or arc known as 'The Donkey's Back' and is a vestige from the original thirteenth-century building. The arc is repeated on St John's pediment.

Next to John's courtyard is another courtyard called **Konventa Seta** or Convent Courtyard, which is now a complex of a hotel, shops, art galleries and cafés and is one of the most beautiful in the city. As you pass through you can see the old city walls on one side and a relief of the Riga coat of arms.

In the restoration of the wall, it was found that grout mixed with dolomite stones was used for the foundation which was laid on sand. The wall itself was built of limestone and faced with bricks. Inside the fortifications, it consisted of two tiers, the lower one in peacetime could be used for storing goods and providing shelter for the homeless. In the Jana Seta the upper part of the wall, the passage, was supported by arches and covered by a wooden roof with tiles. The defenders of the city would stand there and peer through the loopholes at the enemy before they hurled the spears or fired at them with arrows or bullets.

Above: The Presidential reception hall in Riga Castle

Right: Reformed Church built by Kristofers Meinert 1733

Opposite: The arch known as the Donkey's Back, a vestige from the 13th century building

The total height of the wall was about 36ft (11m) and its thickness 8ft (2.5m) at the basement. Whenever the city was in danger various crafts and guilds participated in its preservation, each manning a tower or specific area of the wall.

Konventa Seta was derived from the Holy Spirit Convent which moved here when the first Riga Castle, which had occupied the land, had been destroyed and a new castle had been built on the convent's former site near the river.

The Grey Sisters, an order of Franciscan nuns with a grey habit, took care of the sick, looked after invalids and an additional duty was to educate children. They also had a rule which enabled them to leave the order whenever they chose. The symbol for the Holy Spirit is a dove or pigeon and later, when the buildings were used as warehouses, the bird was adopted by their owners. Consequently, reliefs of doves in different hues were engraved on the buildings.

The courtyard contains a ruin from the old stone structure of the first castle built in 1204 which is now part of the interior of the Hotel Konventa Seta. Fragments of the chapel and assembly hall survived the fire that destroyed it and can be seen in St George's Church which is now part of the Museum of Applied and Decorative Art. It was divided up into three storage areas, the white, the blue and the brown dove and used as such until 1986.

Exit from Konventa Seta in Kalku Street and turn right towards **Philharmonia Square**. When you reach it turn left in Meistaru or Masters' Street. There you will find the two Guilds.

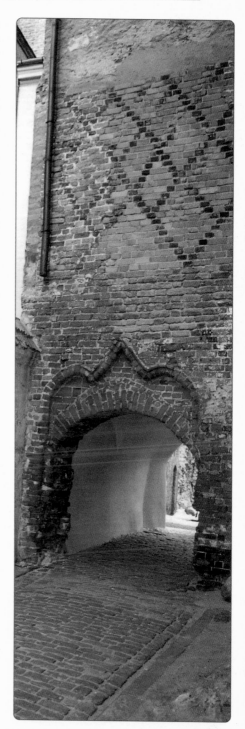

Guild membership

It was not easy to join a guild and once you bought a house in the city, the Town Council put you on the list of either the Great or the Small Guild. However, it was up to the members to admit you. This could create enmity and an anecdote about the Cats' House at 19 Meistaru Street illustrates the point. A Latvian merchant who wanted to become a member of the Great Guild had his application blackballed. As a consequence of the rejection, he placed two black cats on the towers of his building, each with their tails pointing towards the guild. They soon relented and he changed the animals round to more amenable positions.

Associations of Guilds of Craftsmen and Merchants were founded in Riga during the thirteenth century with the purpose of providing charity to their impoverished members and arranging events like funerals and weddings. A great stimulus to trade was Riga's membership of the Hanseatic League from 1282 to 1630, which gave it close ties to the North German cities like Hamburg, Bremen and Lübeck.

Around the fourteenth century, there was a split in the Guild membership and merchants formed a separate branch under the patron of St Mary leaving the craftsmen who were still part of the St Cross and Trinity Guild. In time, as trade grew between the Hanseatic cities, the **Guild of Merchants** became larger, more influential and its members wealthier than the **Craftsmen's Guild**. The members had the monopoly of trade from the East and the West as they alone could sell goods to locals or foreigners.

Amatu or Craft's Street separates the two guilds. If you walk down the street, the Small Guild is on your left and the Great on your right. At the courtyard next to the house at No.4, a fine example of

Wilhelm Bockslaff's Art Nouveau design with men reading books on the roof, there was once a large stone gateway with two entrance arches, one for each guild.

Pious admonition

There were also two plaques attached to the gateway which was removed in the middle of the nineteenth century when restoration work was being carried out. One admonished members to lead a good life. 'Dispense with self-interest and its child, envy; discard luxury and abundance; be industrious; live in harmony and moderation' (and if you accomplish this) with God's help you will live a long life'.

The Small Guild, which with its tower and crenellations looks like a castle, was built in 1866 on the old site and designed by the architect Johann Felsko in what is described as Electic English Gothic style. In the corner of the façade under the little turret is a statue of

St John with a lamb. The link to St John dates back to the thirteenth century when members would congregate in Zosta's room, an old house, which once held the former St John's Chapel and from which the guild derived its coat of arms.

In 1888, the interior decoration of the building was completed and its panelled meeting hall on the first floor is particularly outstanding because of the ornamental ceiling and gallery. Stained glass windows were also installed and many depict craftsmen in their traditional costumes, each with their craft's symbol. One window pays tribute to the architect Johann Felsko and the stained-glass artist, Freidstadte from Hanover. In the same picture is a mother and child with an appropriate caption, 'A good wife and your own hearth is worth gold and pearls'. There are also paintings of scenes from other Hanseatic cities on the walls, as well as a selection of framed common sense and wit to rival Ben Franklin's *Poor Richard's Almanac*. Examples include 'Patience, intelligence and time make the impossible possible.'

The Great Guild was reconstructed a decade earlier than its associate, in 1854 and as the members were loath to lose two original parts they were incorporated by the architect, Karlis Beine, in his English Gothic and Monumental Eclecticism building.

The Minster or Münster room which originates from the thirteenth century and was a Franciscan cloister dining-room decorated with Gothic cross vaults is one element that was preserved and it now serves as a foyer of the **Philharmonic Hall**

(cont'd on page 58)

The famous medieval view found on old maps can be seen from the SAS Radisson hotel across the river

Above: A view of Riga Castle from Vansu Bridge showing the presence of the president whose flag is flying from the Holy Ghost Tower

Below: The panelled meeting hall with ornamental ceiling, stained glass windows and gallery of the Small Guild

Left: the main staircase leading to the meeting hall on the first floor
Right: A portrait of the architect Johann Felsko who designed the Small Guild

which has taken over the Guild building. The derivation of the room's name is doubtful. Some believe it belonged to merchants from the City of Münster, others claim it is an abbreviation of the word monasterium. It was where the money and documents were kept and was also used as an assembly room.

At the upper end is an old carved figure of the Virgin Mary, under which the Chairman sat on public occasions, that was known locally as the Docke, derived from the Danish Dakke or Doll. According to the John Murray travel guide to Russia in 1893, this could well be the origin of 'dock' in the UK Courts of Law.

The other room that was a first choice with the members and has remained unchanged is the Bride's Chamber which was built in the first half of the fifteenth century. It was used during the joyous occasion of a wedding celebration, which lasted several days and had a nuptial bed to which the newly married couple adjourned after they had danced the first dance. On the eve of the wedding two groups of guests, those of the bride and of the groom, drove in coaches through the city twice, each time to the beat of drums and the blowing of trumpets. There is no record of whether the sheets were shown from the windows to the jovial guests the next day!

The square chamber was constructed with richly ornamental star vaults and there is an inscription on the fireplace no doubt for the edification of the couple. 'Do not say things that please people, but speak about things which are of benefit to society'.

We end our walk by following Meistaru Street to the intersection where we began our tour. As a preview of the next tour of the Art Noveau architecture you may wish to stroll down Smilsu Street which is a reminder that the city originated on a sandy peninsula which arose from the Daugava, and its tributary the Ridzene, which has since been filled in. Its outline can still be seen in Kaleju Street.

Since the thirteenth century this street was the most important because it was the continuation of Smilsu Road and sited at the oldest entrance to the city. It is certainly one of the few that has retained its name from earliest times.

Smilsu Road was the main thoroughfare from the countryside and linked villages on the Daugava with the Liv and Latgallian castles on the Gauja river and the craftsmen's settlements around the castle walls. Some stretches were paved with limestone flags, and yards along the way with round timber.

During the middle ages Smilsu Street had two public wells and a coal market. Although little of the medieval architecture has remained the street has become a showcase for Art Nouveau styles from 1902 to 1910 and includes the most prominent practitioners such as Konstantis Peksens (at No.2), Wilhelm Bockslaff (at No.6), Heinrich Scheel (at No.8) and Ernests Pole (at No.10).

There are examples too of the master of Eclecticism, Johann Felsko at No's.7 and 12 and the famous Kristofers Haberland has an apartment house at No.5.

TOUR TWO: ART NOUVEAU

The Art Nouveau tour covers both the old town and the new city. It is not feasible to see all the buildings and on this walk we will concentrate on the flashy, the elegant and on as many variations of the style as possible.

We begin in **Peitavas Street** with a place of worship, a synagogue, which was the first example of the Perpendicular style and was built in 1904 from the design of the architect and art historian Wilhelm Neumann. It is best seen from the front and although austere in comparison with other buildings the pediment design is successfully echoed in the canopy above the main door and on the side above the two windows; perpendicular derived from the style applied to the Wertheim department store in Berlin.

Moving towards **Kaleju Street**, we turn left into it and follow it round until we reach a ritzy building No.23 which is on the corner with **Jana Street**. The architect,

Paul Mandelstamm, who was a leading figure in Eclecticism, Art Nouveau and a pioneer in Functionalism was prolific with buildings to his credit in the city.

Head down Teatra Street and turn right into Richard Wagner or **Vagnera** as it is known in Latvian. There you will find the concert hall in which he conducted and a second hand bookshop that has a small selection of English books. Soon we turn into the main street **Kalku** and later turn right into **Skunu** where again we find the duo, Scheel and Scheffel's building at No.10/12. Here you can experience the basic definition of the style, according to Louis Sullivan the floral, the sway, the swirl, the intertwine, the 'elegant' and the

A preference

In **Teatra Street** (from Kaleju Street) you will find my preferred building designed by architects Scheel and Scheffel which now belongs to the **Italian Embassy** at No.9. I have to admit that I was not attracted to Art Nouveau at first because I thought it was too elaborate, fussy, excessive but was gradually won over and a turning point was seeing this building from the vantage point of the fifth floor of the Riga Hotel. I had noticed the blue globe glowing at night and was entranced when I saw it in the morning light with sun moving from the globe to the silver rounded tower of the building opposite. Swallows circled in fast flight around this duo and I saw movement in these architectural forms. A strong feature is the cardinal cap roof under the three Atlas figures and the window with arched eyebrow.

TOUR 2:
ART NOUVEAU

Daugava

KEY

Regeneration area of
the Old Town

—— 1863-1900. Eclecticism

—— 1900-1914. Art-Nouveau

—— 1928-1939. Modern

① W. Neumann	1904	
② P. Mandelstamm	1903	
③ H. Scheel & F. Scheffel	1903	
④ H. Scheel & F. Scheffel	1902	
⑤ K. Peksens	1902	
⑥ H. Scheel & F. Scheffel	1902	
⑦ A. Moedlinger & H. Zeiberlich	1910	
⑧ E. Laube	1912	
⑨ E. Laube	1909	
⑩ E. Laube	1908	
⑪ W. Neumann	1900	
⑫ A. Schmaeling	1903	
⑬ H. Hartmann	1907	
⑭ A. Malvess	1910	
⑮ H. Scheel & F. Scheffel	1901	
⑯ M. Eisenstein	1903	
⑰ M. Eisenstein	1906	
⑱ M. Eisenstein	1904	
⑲ M. Eisenstein	1903	
⑳ M. Eisenstein	1903	
㉑ E. Laube	1908	
㉒ M. Eisenstein	1905	
㉓ M. Nuksa	1911	
㉔ R. Zirkwitz	1899	

graceful; a luxurious decoration on the eclectic façade.

Proceed down Skunu, skirt the Dome Square and turn right into **Smilsu**, which has several good examples. At No.2 we find the first of our two erotic buildings, with a Brunnhilde on the left and her bearded King Gunther on the right. It is such eroticism that distinguishes Latvian art from its European equivalent. It is designed by Konstantins Peksens the most

prolific Rigan architect who produced some 250 buildings in the city! The peacock is an interesting feature as well as the spiky witches' hat on the roof.

The building on the corner with **Aldaru**, No.8, has two female nudes holding an accolade perhaps for the two architects Scheel and Scheffel who designed it as it is one of their finest. Look closely at the main door as it is a fine calling card for the building's style and the reliefs which are finely executed by another duo, sculptors called Otto and Wassil. The wrought-iron work above the main entrance at roof level and on the two sides is extremely unusual.

The interior is resplendent and of particular note are women dressed in Empire-Style loose fitting clothes. When you come to the corner where Maza Smilsu intersects, look and you will find the black cat sculpture on the tower. The building, on that corner is No.3, which contains the Parex Bank, and is one of the few that can be entered. It was designed by architects Adolf Moedlinger and Helmut Zeiberlich.

The next stage of the tour takes us into the new city and extends over a wide area including Alberta Street where the most outstanding examples are found. From the top of Smilsu Street we turn right into **Aspazijas Boulevard** and at the **Laima Clock** move towards the Freedom Monument, the most sacred spot for Latvians. The clock is a popular meeting place for lovers. We move around the monument which is in Brivibas Boulevard and towards the Esplanade on our left.

Left: Fine decorative work on a building designed by Mikhail Eisenstein in 1903 at 10A Elizabetes Street

Above: One of the first Art Nouveau buildings in Riga designed by Alfred Aschenkampff in 1899, 7 Audeju Street

Wagner connection

The first Art Nouveau building is No.33, at the corner of **Brivibas** and **Dzirnavu**, which has a special significance to music lovers as it was built on the site of a former house where Wagner spent two years *(see Music entry)*. Designed by one of the pioneers of the style, Eizens Laube, the building is rather dark as the façade is clad in black labradorite and is another example of the vertical architecture.

The apartment block at No.37 is also designed by Laube but in the National Romanticism style. Of note is the relief depicting a trio of owls, a triangular balcony and the unusual tiled effect of the peaked roof. The third building by Laube in the street at the corner of Lacplesa Street, No.47, is one of the most outstanding examples of National Romanticism he designed.

One of the first Art Nouveau buildings in the suburbs is found at No.55. A bright orange façade with variations of Dutch gables including one, above the main entrance, with two scrolls. It was built in 1900 and designed by Wilhelm Neumann. The reliefs are the work of Andris Volz.

On the opposite corner at No.68 is a building designed by Alexander Schmaeling three years later, and which attempted to synchronize with No.55 and create an ensemble. There is an interplay of gables and the fine decorative effects on each building complement each other. But the tower

with its resemblance to the Dome's tower is no match for the gable with the twin scrolls. The tower with its onion top that can only be seen from several stories up is its most striking feature.

It is at this corner that we turn left down Getrudes Street towards Valdemara. (For those who have been truly bitten by the bug of this architectural style, they may want to walk over three blocks to No.85 and look at Laube's musical masterpiece before joining us again).

When you reach **Valdemara** you turn off into it and head towards No.20. This is quite a conservative building designed by Hermann Hartmann in 1907 and the interesting feature is the use of a band of tiles at the bottom of the low gables. Although the building next door at No.18 is small, its National Romanticism design is effective and should be seen from across the street where it is most striking, particularly the two cowl-like or hooded windows at the top that form part of the roof. The architect was Augusts Malvess and it was built in 1910.

On the way to Elizabetes Street we pass another Scheel and Schaffel building at No.23 the door of which is a splendid example of the use of ironwork in Art Nouveau.

From Elizabetes Street we come to the corner at Antonijas Street and turn right into it before taking the first left into **Alberta Street** which is a highlight of our Art Nouveau tour. Of the five Eisenstein buildings we will see, four of which are in this street, No.2 is the most beautiful. Built in 1906, the last one in Alberta, it appears to have benefited from his

First sight of Eisenstein design

In **Elizabetes Street** we get a foretaste of the grandeur that will come later. At No.10b we see the first brilliant design of Mikhail Eisenstein and its theatrical façade. If there is someone who shines in this style it is him. The use of the blue tiles and the Aztec heads to crown the balustrade of the roof are prominent features. In the original drawing, the tiles on the two top floors were red, a tone which was not used in the end as it would not have been as effective. However, he does use red to great advantage later.

experience. The use of the red tile stripes resembles festive ribbons and provides it with an air of celebration. The five round holes at the top of the façade are like windows open to the sky and on a clear day add blue which he so likes.

Additional effects of the five knights with their visors, up on the uppermost façade and the two sphinxes below, guarding the main entrance, give the building a forceful presence. Two topless belles balance the masculinity. The common part of the interior does not let the exterior down and the décor is soft and graceful to complement it. It is worth entering and the door is usually open. (It is the birthplace of Sir Isaiah Berlin.)

The building at No.4 is a plain version of his style and has great strength in an oval shaped window just below the ovoid pediment with

its rampant lions on either side. No tiles are used to embellish it and it should be best seen from across the street. The semi-circular top façade is a particularly successful feature of Art Nouveau such as on Smilsu 3 and Brivibas 72. It was built in 1904, a year before the other two buildings in the street. These were No's.6 and 8, built at the same time, but No.6 appears to fall short of the mark if compared to its sketch which is superior. Perhaps, in the rush to complete both, a wrong decision was made to use red bricks on the façade rather than red tiles which would have been more effective. This can be seen clearly in their use in No.8 where the turquoise tiles brighten the building and make it more prominent than its square box structure would project.

Laube's building at No.11 demonstrates through its gloomy, austere exterior how much of a genius Eisenstein was.

On the way back to Elizabetes Street via **Strelnieku Street** you will see another Eisenstein at No.4a which although elaborate in decorative effects does not surpass any of his masterpieces in Alberta. At No.2, there is another example of how differently this style was expressed in Riga. It was designed by Martins Nuksa in 1911. He was also an ambassador for Latvia who like the architect Mandelstamm met with a tragic end. The top of the façade with crenellations gives an impression of a Spanish fort.

The last stop on the tour is at the corner of Vilandes Street, No.1, a fine example of the early style by Rudolf Zirkwitz. It has been beautifully restored.

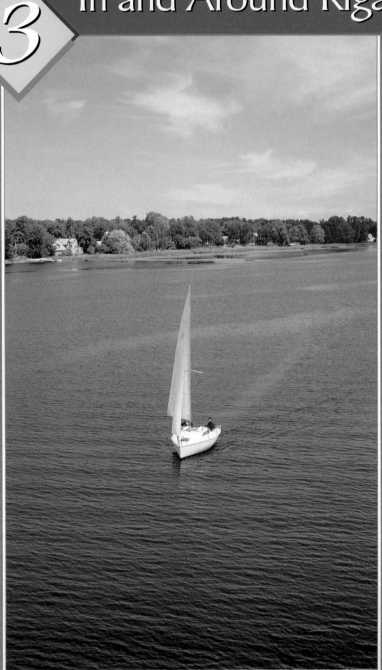

> eaving aside the middle of the city, there are a number of places very close by which are of interest. Perhaps one of the most surprising is the coast.

The seaside – Jurmala

Jurmala, which means seaside in Latvian, is one of the secrets about Riga that the Russians knew, that is only now filtering through to the West. The Latvian Riviera is a spectacular wild coast with pine trees bordering on the sandy beaches, where during summer bathers can frolic in the water until evening because of the midnight sun.

Unlike the French and Italian Rivieras, which are built-up areas with promenades and high rises, Jurmala, has the innocence of the African coast. If you are lucky you might find a lone ice-cream cart or a few canvas covered cafés along its 25-mile (45km) long stretch of golden sands.

A geographical feature similar to Miami beach is a river, the Lielupe, running parallel to the shore except for a couple of places when it loops away or inward towards the beach at the main villages Majori and Dubulti. Here the strip of land is only 500yd (457m) wide.

The resort which traces its origins to 1738 when sea bathing was first recorded, consists of a string of fifteen villages. Priedaine is first and nearest to Riga and is

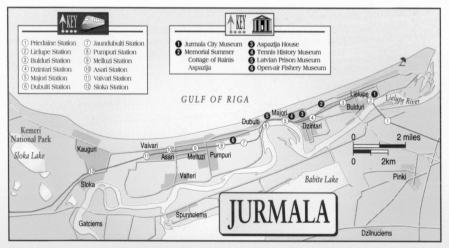

KEY
① Priedaine Station
② Lielupe Station
③ Bulduri Station
④ Dzintari Station
⑤ Majori Station
⑥ Dubulti Station
⑦ Jaundubulti Station
⑧ Pumpuri Station
⑨ Melluzi Station
⑩ Asari Station
⑪ Vaivari Station
⑫ Sloka Station

KEY
❶ Jurmala City Museum
❷ Memorial Summer Cottage of Rainis Aspazija
❸ Aspazija House
❹ Tennis History Museum
❺ Latvian Prison Museum
❻ Open-air Fishery Museum

GULF OF RIGA

Kemeri National Park

Sloka Lake

Kauguri

Vaivari

Asari

Melluzi

Pumpuri

Valteri

Sloka

Gatciems

Spunnciems

Dubulti

Majori

Dzintari

Lielupe

Bulduri

Lielupe River

Babite Lake

Pinki

Dzilnuciems

0   2 miles

0   2km

JURMALA

located on the banks of the Lielupe river. Here there is an anchorage for yachts. It was built as a residential village for railway workers on the Riga-Orla line. The others Lielupe, Bulduri, Dzintari, Majori, Dubulti, Jaundubulti (new Dubulti), Pumpuri, Melluzi, Asari and Vaivari are on the peninsula between the sea and the river. Sloka Kemeri and Jaunkemeri (new Kemeri) are near the sea and the Sloka lake.

Each village has its own character. **Majori** is the liveliest with cafés, art galleries and shops. **Dzintari**, previously called Edinburgh was popular with aristocrats, and its name originated when Maria, the daughter of Tsar Alexander II married the Duke of Edinburgh. At its western end is the summer concert hall, built in 1936 with wall paintings by a local artist Ansis Cirulis, which was extended to include an open-air auditorium.

Lielupe has a yacht club and is a sports complex with tennis courts where Davis Cup matches have been held. There are good examples of houses in National Romanticism and Functionalism styles. Due to its remoteness from main villages it was called Australia. **Melluzi**, which is also called Karlsbad after the monocled

Baron Firks who owned this village and Majori, is a quiet small place like **Asari** and **Vaivari**, which has an aquatic amusement park.

Dubulti was also the site of the Jewish quarter where Osip Mandelstam would spend holidays with his grandparents. The area between Dubulti and Melluzi was marshy and when it was developed as **Jaundubulti**, wood and gravel was used to strengthen the ground.

Kemeri, which is inland, and **Jaunkemeri**, which is on the bay, are traditional therapeutic places. This is another unique feature of Jurmala for it has been known as a spa and health complex from the time it was opened as a sea resort. Kemeri, which is 4 miles (6km) from the sea, has sulphur springs amongst the surrounding swamps and the locals used the 'holy springs' for medicinal purposes. Foresters first administered the treatment in the healing waters and one of them, Kemers, gave his name to the area.

There is a third compelling reason to visit the Riga seaside – to see examples of the striking wooden architecture both of the nineteenth and twentieth centuries. Of these, 428 buildings have been declared monuments and been included on the project list of UNESCO's world cultural heritage.

Russian convalescents

Dubulti is one of the oldest fisherman's villages in Riga bay and during the Napoleonic wars, officers and wounded soldiers would come here to recuperate. Among them was the famous Russian general, Barclay de Tollay who was responsible for the strategy which defeated Napoleon. There was a statue of him on the Esplanade but now only the plinth remains.

Mandelstam's bustling noisy life has found a place in posterity.

Visitors to the seaside first stayed with the local fishermen and farmers who added extensions like terraces and top floors, but during the middle of the nineteenth century, summer cottages were built, particularly when river boat services between Riga and Jurmala gave easy access. The demand for cottages grew after the railway was built in 1877 and gave an impetus to new villages such as Edinburgh, Jaundubulti and Bulduri.

The architectural style during the nineteenth century can be identified by classical elements like columns, pilasters, cornices and pediments. An example of this style can be found in Majori at 43 Jomas Street. The one-floor symmetrical house with monumental columns creates an atmosphere of solemnity but fits in well with the other buildings in the square it faces.

It should be compared with a set of houses on 52-54 Dzintaru Avenue in Dzintari. The main building is a Neo-Gothic asymmetrical structure with turrets, loggias and the unpractical flat roof. The owner, Kristaps Morbergs, added an unusual dimension by covering the wooden framework with copper plates which cause the house to glow at sunset.

A fisherman's cottage built in the early part of the nineteenth century can be seen in Dubulti at 15 Blaumana Street. There is another old example in the same street at No.7 which is crowned with a pediment, classical wooden columns and a semi-circular window.

The most popular style of dacha is Art Nouveau which is usually asymmetrical, frequently adorned by turrets with iron weathercocks bearing the initial of the owner. A signature of the style is embodied in the **Hotel Majori** which was built in 1925 at 25 Jomas Street and designed by Artur Medlinger. Although purists would argue that the stripes on the first floor typify Classicism and other parts smack of Neo-Baroque, it is nevertheless a good illustration. Another early building is 58 Strelnieku Avenue, (lit 3) Jaundubulti.

There are several other styles like 'Homeland' which derive from Germany (131 Meza Avenue, Lielupe); Neo-Classicism, (2 Juras Steet, Majori), and Romanticism that was stimulated by Latvia's independence (3 Rotas Street, Lielupe). One can see the famous example of the Kemeri hotel (25 Darzina Street, Kemeri) which is one of the most beautiful hotels in Latvia and situated in a landscaped park with garden pavilions, canals, bridges and pathways. Finally there is Neo-Renaissance (3 Valnu Street, Bulduri); Neo-Russian (4 Arijas Street, Asari); Neo-Gothic (Morberg's House, 50152 Dzintaru) and Functionalism (8 Kronvalda Street and 28 Melluza Aveunue, Melluzu).

For readers who enjoy an architectural feast I recommend the book *Architectural Heritage of Jurmala Part 1*, which is written by Richard Petersons and Anita Naudisa.

Most of these buildings have been frozen in time for over fifty years and now are gradually being

(cont'd on page 70)

Above: Formerly used for spa treatment, eclectic Art Nouveau style, Majori

Below: An example of national romanticism with a thatched roof in Kemeri, 1933

Opposite top: Kemeri National Park with sulphur ponds and wetlands

Opposite bottom: Horse riding on Vaivari beach

• JURMALA •
SPA & HEALTH RESORT

There are over thirty springs in Kemeri. Once the mineral waters were examined chemically in St Petersburg, the first state bathing establishment was opened in 1838 through a grant of land by Tsar Nicholas I. Sapropelic mud, which consists of decomposing organic matter, was subsequently discovered in the Kanieris Lake and is also used in treatments like slimming.

Since then the whole area has become a health resort with over thirty spa hotels offering a variety of rejuvenating cures and thalassotherapies. Many of the hotels have doctors and medical facilities. The mild climate, medicinal mud and sulphurous mineral water combine to make it popular for rest and recreation. The Russian cosmonauts would stay at Vaivari where a special spa was built for them.

It is not unusual for guests to stay for two to three months to undergo treatment or spa cures while on holiday. For example, at the Marienbade in Majori, cardio-vascular and gynaecological diseases are treated as well as metabolic disorders and problems of the nervous system. For as little as £6 or $10 a day the guest can have a consultation with a doctor, mud treatment, medical baths and showers, physiotherapy and acupuncture.

At the Vaivari, which is also the National Rehabilitation Centre, both spa medicine and spa cures are offered. The medical side includes paediatrics, children's orthopaedic surgery, traumatology, neurology, cardiology, plastic surgery and dietology. According to Dr Gundars Rusovs, it is ideal for patients to recuperate after operations, or in the case of stroke victims to help them back to leading as near as possible a normal life. There is a hydro and physiotherapy complex where medical baths, mud procedures and other physical fitness methods are carried out.

I had a water massage, which is unlike any other physiotherapy. You enter a bath twice the size of a normal one, which is filled with warm brownish-hued mineral water. A female attendant runs a hose with water under pressure over your body underwater and the flesh gives way. It is a strange sensation and becomes ticklish when applied to the soles of the feet.

renovated. However, there has been a recent new addition designed by a top international architect Meinhard von Gerkan who was born in Riga and has a practice in Hamburg. It has all the hallmarks of a Von Gerkan, Marg and Partners building, whether it be a music and conference hall in Lubeck, an airport in Algiers or Hamburg. In essence, there is present a dome or atrium, a textural effect on steel, concrete or glass and an example of modernism in architecture.

The building was commissioned by Victor Krasovitsky and has been described as a deconstructivist Bauhaus house that fits in well with the other dachas as it is a wooden structure. Siberian larch is used outside and interior cupboards, bookshelves and panels are constructed out of cherry wood.

An interesting feature is that it serves as the guest house to an Italianate Villa Marta in which the banker lives. As he likes this particular architectural style, everything in the new house from lamps to furniture is reproduction Bauhaus. The surprise for guests is the central atrium which is an open space for parties. There is a music room with a Steinway grand for concerts, an art gallery with paintings by Malevich, Kandinsky and Miro, a cinema with a huge screen and a library. Outside, between the two houses, is a Japanese garden.

Although the house was primarily planned for visitors, Victor Krasovitsky finds that he and his wife Nina tend to spend more and more time in it because of the interesting interior spaces.

Kemeri National Park

For the tourist who can easily forego beaches and boring buildings but goes weak at the knees at the sight of rare birds, animals and plants then the Kemeri National Park is their place.

It is an amazing nature reserve that includes **Kemeri** and **Jaunkemeri** with wetlands, forests, lakes, villages, lagoons and stretches of coast land. As embodied under law, the area is under state protection and established to maintain the natural, cultural, historical and balneological values and protect the processes of the origin of mineral waters and medicinal mud.

The source of the sulphurous springs was the result of the interaction between dolomite primary rock and a large marsh complex. Another interesting element is the geological structures that connect at this point. Due to the rise of land, the ancient Littorina sea retreated leaving dunes, and coastal lagoons.

Diverse ecosystems maintain the biological diversity of plants and animals. Some twenty-five per cent of the plant species in the Latvian Red data book are found here. This includes 521 types of fungi, 139 lichens, 202 mosses and 894 plants. In the wet forests, spurge, honeysuckle and ramson are found and in the coastal area the great fen sedge, brown bog-rush and bog myrtle. Orchids flourish too in the fens, the early marsh orchid, and the heath spotted orchid among others.

(cont'd on page 74)

Memorial Summer Cottage of Rainis & Aspazija
5/7 Plieksana Street, Majori
Open 10am-5pm Monday to Sunday, closed Tuesday.
☎ 776 4295

Jurmala City Museum
27/29 Tirgona Street, Majori
An art museum with representative works of Latvian artists from the past and present. Open 11am-5pm Wednesday to Sunday, closed Monday & Tuesday.
☎ 776 4746

Aspazija House
20 Meierovica Avenue, Dubulti
Open 11am-4pm Tuesday, Wednesday, Thursday and Saturday, 2-7pm Monday, closed Friday and Sunday.
☎ 776 9445

Jurmala Tennis History Museum
50/52 Strelnieku Avenue, Jaundubulti
Open 9am-8pm Monday to Sunday. ☎ 776 9254

Latvian Prison Museum
6/8 Piestatnes Street, Dzintari
History of prisons from the Middle Ages to the present. Open 9am-8pm Monday to Friday, closed Saturday & Sunday. ☎ 775 4536

Open-air Fishery Museum
An unusual excursion to see old fishermans' cottages and fishing equipment, and a trip around a fish factory combined with food tasting. Open 10am-6pm daily.
☎ 775 1121

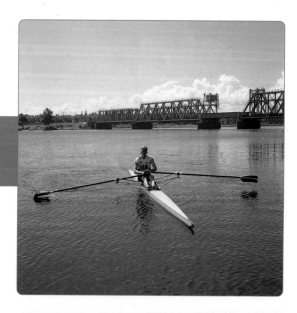

A racing scull on the Lielupe River near the railway bridge

'*Welcome to our unspoilt beaches and 20 miles of fine sand*'

Jurmala City Council,
1/5 Jomas Street, Jurmala-LV-2015, Latvia
Phone: +371 7093800. Fax: +371 7762288
Web-site: http://.Jurmala.lv E-mail: vilniss@jpd.gov.lv

Mayor Leonids Alksnis

It is also home to over 200 species of birds including the magnificent eagle owl, the white tailed eagle and the whimbrel along the seashore. This should place it as a significant site on the birdwatcher circuit.

Good breeding conditions have encouraged the presence of the black stork which is considered to be a lucky bird in Latvia and special nesting attachments are placed on roofs even at Rundale to attract them *(see page 100)*. The common crane which belies its name as it is not often seen, the lesser spotted eagle and great numbers of the shy corncrakes which are heard rather than seen.

The undisturbed virgin forests have also provided shelter for rare species of woodpeckers – three-toed, middle-spotted and white-backed as well as animals like the wolf, the wild boar, the roe deer and the red deer. Eurasian beaver flourish in the wet areas and the elk prefers the marshes.

Entomologists too will have a field day as there are over 3,000 insect varieties on the site. With wild species of plants and animals disappearing every year worldwide, the Kemeri National Park is a rare place to visit and the scenery is spectacular, particularly the sulphur ponds, boat station and wetlands which from the air look similar to the Okavango deltas.

It is easy to reach from Riga as commuter trains stop at Kemeri station and the Information Centre which is located at the Forest House or **Meza maja** is only a short bus ride away. The address: Meza maja, Kemeri, Jurmala LV-2012, ☎ 776 5386, Fax 776 5040, E-mail kemeri@vdc.lv.

Cultural life of Jurmala

Jurmala, the seaside of Riga, has a lot to offer the visitor and is within half an hour of the city, depending on where you stay. Some may wish to make it their base.

Cultural activities are carried out on a minor scale compared to the city. For businessmen who

(cont'd on page 78)

Adolf Zardinsh

One artist found Jurmala's climate (the sunniest place in Latvia) and ambience so much to his liking that he spent thirty years in exile here, from 1937 to 1967, after being turned down as a member of the Art Society in Riga. He was a proficient linguist and spoke English, French and German, besides Latvian and Russian, and filled his diary with comments in any of these languages. Another mainstay during those decades when he dedicated his life totally to art, was his perfect knowledge of the world history of art. Adolf Zardinsh was born in Riga, grew up in Vitesk and retired in solitude to Jurmala. The harder his life became, the more he was inspired by painting and when his works were discovered in an attic in 1997, there were no less than 1,500 paintings he had left to posterity. Be warned how seductive the area is!

• THE RIGA SEASIDE •

As a child, the eminent Russian poet Osip Mandelstam
(1891-1938) would be taken by his parents to the
Latvian Riviera at the turn of the century. He has a vivid
memory of these holidays and has described them in his
prose work the *Noise of Time.*

'The Riga seaside is an entire country in itself. It is famed for
its oozy, pure yellow and astonishingly fine sand (even in an
hourglass one could hardly find such sand!) and also for the
little boardwalks consisting of one or two hole-riddled planks
that had been thrown across the 20 versts (Russian unit of
measurement) of the villa-dotted Sahara.

'There are no watering places anywhere that can compare
with the swing and scope of the dacha life along the Riga
coast. The boardwalks, flowerbeds, enclosed front gardens,
and decorative glass balls stretch out in a huge endless city,
all on a yellow, finely milled, canary sand, such as children
play with.

'In the backyards Latvians dry and cure flounder, a one-eyed
bony fish, flat as a broad palm. The wailing children, piano
scales, the groans of patients from the innumerable dentists'
offices, the clatter or crockery in the little resort pensions, the
roulades of singers and the shouts to the peddlers – these
noises are never silenced in the labyrinth of kitchen gardens,
bakeries and barbed wire, and as far as the eye can see along
the sand embankment run little toy trains, shod with rails and
filled to overflowing with 'hares' who leap about during the trip
from prim German Bilderlingshof to congested Jewish
Dubbeln, which smelled of swaddling clothes. Wandering
musicians strolled about among the sparse pine groves; two
convoluted trumpets, a clarinet, and a trombone. Forever
being chased away, they blow out their mercilessly false brass
note and now here, now there, strike up the equestrian march
of the splendid Karolina. (Hares are people who leap on and
off moving trams to avoid paying fares.)

'The whole region was controlled by a monocled baron
named Firks. He divided his land into two parts; that which
had been cleaned of Jews and that which had not. In the clean
half, German students sat scraping their beer steins about on
small tables. In the Jewish section babies' diapers hung from
lines, and piano scales would gasp for breath. In the Germans'
Majorenhof there were concerts: Strauss's *Death and
Transfiguration* played by a symphony orchestra in the shell in
the park. Elderly German women, their cheeks glowing and
their mourning freshly donned found it consoling.

'In Jewish Dubbeln the orchestra strained at Tchaikovsky's
Symphonie Pathetique and one could hear the two nests of
strings calling back and forth to each other.'

Dzintari beach

want to unwind and have fun there is plenty to choose from including tennis, riding, fishing, water sports, yachting, sailing, water-skiing, rowing and hunting. The **Latvian Hunting and Fishing Club** is a good contact and it recommends **Lake Babite**, near Jurmala for fishing. They have a boat that can be hired.

Several museums are spread over six villages and although interesting, the collections are small.

In Majori, the pride of place is the **Memorial Summer Cottage** of the famous Latvian poet, Janis Rainis (1865-1929) and his feminist wife, also a poet, Elza Rozenberga (1865-1943) aka Aspazija. It is a spacious house and also has art Nouveau exhibits, the most spectacular of which is a clock with a nude female sculpture.

Aspazija lived in another house in the next village, Dubulti, for the last ten years of her life. She wrote, "Work is the main nerve of my life. It is my spring revival." A visit there will be interesting as three other noteworthy buildings No's. 20, 36 and 38 are listed on the same avenue, Z Meierovica.

In keeping with the Latvian's oddball choice of museums, Jurmala has one on tennis, another on prisons, a third on the fishing industry and one devoted to a minor literary figure, Ludins Berzins in Jaundubulti.

The Brothers' Cemetery

I have never visited a military cemetery, as there was never a compelling reason to go. None of my relatives were buried in one and photographs I had seen of Arlington or Normandy depicted rows and rows of neat white crosses, which were off-putting for seeing the real thing. When the Brothers' Cemetery was suggested as a sight, I demurred even though the Latvian Tourist Office tried to persuade me of its worthiness by mentioning that it was a fixture on all Finnish tours. I had heard of the Finns' bibulous nature but not of their interest in morbid things, unless of course they used the visit as an excuse to imbibe more vodka.

However, my curiosity was aroused and as the site was on the way to our destination, the Ethnographic Museum, I agreed to a short stop, particularly as Anda Rezgale, the guide, assured me that there were no graves in the cemetery. If that was the case, I asked myself, why have it?

To be precise, it is an architectural monument, filled with trees and sculptures, and constructed during the heady days of the country's independence. For the first time in several hundred years the nation was free and to celebrate they built the Freedom Monument in the middle of Riga.

The place is more than a commemoration to soldiers who died in both world wars and fighting for independence. It is an expression of the Latvian culture and beliefs.

When Christianity was first brought to the inhabitants of the country by Bishop Albert in the late thirteenth century, he found that they tended to congregate in groves of oak trees to worship. To discourage what he termed pagan practices he cut down all these sacred trees, which also represented men and strength.

The cemetery lies on the outskirts of the city and is easily reached by bus (No.4 or 9) from Brivibas or tram (No.11) from the National Opera stop. It is always open.

You enter the Brothers' rectangular park through an open stone gateway with a carved relief of horsemen on both sides. Their heads hang low as do the regimental flags they carry. Two European lime or linden trees stand on either side of the gateway near the horsemen. According to Latvians, these trees are symbols of females.

The first thing you glimpse as you walk in, is the huge female statue at the other end of the park, which is 500yd (457m) away. As you move towards the series of steps at the halfway mark, you notice a colonnade of fifty oak trees on either side of the wide carpet of cut grass. You mount the staircase to find an altar in which an eternal flame has been placed. Here you pause and look down and understand that the cemetery has been designed on two levels.

Anda points below and says 'Aizsaule' which translated from Latvian means aftersun or the area that describes the place inhabited by the dead. There is no heaven or earth in Latvian beliefs but sun and aftersun.

Mother Latvia is still far away and at her feet lie the two brothers, back to back. The figures are mounted on a wall which is decorated with the coats of arms of all the towns. You move down the steps into a rectangular enclosure, a low wall which is covered with hundreds of square dull plaques with names and dates of soldiers killed during the various wars.

There are also some 300 blank plaques for the unknown soldiers who died in the World War II. Again, you see reliefs of horsemen at the point of death, when they have taken a bullet, an arrow or sword thrust to the heart and the horse arcs its neck sensing something strange has happened to the rider. We return at a slow pace and by the time we pass through the gateway, we have walked 1,000yd (1km).

The brief period of independence, a mere two decades, came to an end in 1939 and post-war Latvia became occupied by the Soviet Union. To Sovietise the memorial site, twenty-three Soviet soldiers were buried in the cemetery in 1958. When independence was achieved for a second time, these corpses were removed and the site has become a focus for mass demonstrations every 14 June, the date that commemorates the Stalinist deportations.

As you will see from the Dainas, or songs, Latvian culture customs and beliefs cannot be simply ascribed to paganism. A visit here is a good start to understanding the people, and a moving one. Both the sculptures here and the Freedom Monument are the work of Karlis Zale.

The Freedom Monument

The other national shrine is Milda, the nickname for the Freedom Monument, which was finished in 1935, a year before the Brothers' cemetery. Sited on the edge of the Old City at the Junction of Brivibas and Raina Boulevard this *(cont'd on page 82)*

Above: Jurmala Beach

Below left: A sculpture of Mother Latvia at the Brothers' Cemetery

Below right: A typical wooden summer cottage built at the beginning of the 20th century, Jurmala

The Freedom Monument

Defending the monument

The Soviet authorities attempted to take down the monument on several occasions but the Rigans protected it vigorously against such action. They then resorted to other tactics and allowed traffic to move around the monument and made it illegal for the locals to approach it. Some did and placed flowers at the base, an act that resulted in deportation to Siberia or loss of jobs.

is another expression of exuberance during the heady days of Independence, it is the Latvians' equivalent of the Statue of Liberty.

There is no torch in her right hand or tablet in her left, nor a poem extolling the tired, the poor and the huddled masses; but Milda instead holds three golden stars aloft, each representing a province of the country with an inscription reading 'for Fatherland and Freedom'. The tall, long-legged figure accurately depicts the types of females you find in the city.

It is a focal point on 18th November, National Independence Day, where the Prime Minister and President review the armed forces. Friezes around the square base show ordinary men and women singing and working while soldiers fight for freedom. Two guards of honour stand to attention at the front of the base. Milda, which occupies the former site of a statue of Peter the Great who had bought a house in the city, is hollow inside and it is possible to walk up

to the top where a window offers a splendid view. However, the entrance is closed.

Salaspils Concentration Camp Memorial

When I was told that I was going to stay as a guest with a famous Latvian writer, who lived in Salaspils, I was somewhat dismayed. This was the site of a former Nazi concentration camp. I imagined that the town, some 9 miles (15km) south-east of Riga, was close to the camp and that the buildings would resemble those of Auschwitz and Belsen. I was mistaken on both counts. The town was nowhere near the camps, which had been carefully hidden by the Nazis in a forest, and all the buildings had been razed to the ground. The camp can be reached by train, alighting at Darzinia station and following a footpath for about fifteen minutes.

The memorial erected on the site of the camp is both dramatic, and successful as outdoor sculpture. Other holocaust monuments in the US and Europe are different and not as effective because they are too abstract and minimalist in their conception. Here both the figurative and abstract elements work harmoniously and the horror of the event is etched on your mind through giant statues in a simple way. The titles are meaningful; the broken, the humiliated, solidarity and Mother Latvia.

A naked woman, so often seen in snapshots, on private film of the executions taken by soldiers, is shown kneeling. You see the outline of her back and buttocks and the Linden tree planted nearby partly covers her body for modesty. In the foreground, to the right is a man lying on the ground with his torso slightly raised. Such a stance reveals an unbroken spirit even as he lies dying. Behind him in the background, stand three men; one with his fists raised while another supports a weaker colleague. Then right at the back of this group, situated in 99 acres (40 hectares), stands a defiant Mother Latvia. Not in a consoling role as she is in the Brothers' Cemetery, but confronting the threat to her people, who, as children, shelter behind her.

An abstract counterpoint to these figures is an oblong black marble block which is positioned some way in front of the kneeling woman. As I strolled in this Gulliver landscape on a warm sunny day in May enthralled by it all, I was disturbed by a knocking sound. It was a pesky sound of a hammer on stone. I looked for the source, but only saw a woman placing flowers on a gravestone in an adjacent cemetery, and then as I moved towards the marble block, I then understood that the sound emanated from a hole in the stone. The penny dropped, this was a buried metronome.

I soon forgot about the irritant when I saw a little daisy-chain garland, and four bunches of flowers including red carnations, lying against the dark stone. A beautiful and poignant reminder of a loving link with the past.

The entrance to this field of giants is under a long concrete block half sunken into the earth at one end and resting up against a huge black base at the other. There are many notches in the base, and the only explanation I have is that each notch represents a day of the camps existence. Black letters are written across the angled concrete block and are from a Latvian poet, Eizens Veveris, who was imprisoned there. 'Behind this entrance the earth moans'.

On the way back, I found steps inside the block which led to a view at the top, when you exited at the bottom to a small display of about ten illustrations of different parts of the camp. There were thirty-nine barracks on the site between 1941-1944 where Jews and other prisoners of war were murdered. Salaspils was one of several labour camps and stones mark the perimeter.

4

City Art Galleries & Museums

There is a wide range of museums and art galleries in Riga. Details of locations and opening times for all those mentioned here can be found in the panel at the end of this chapter.

ART IN LATVIA

Art ranks high in Latvian culture which has produced notable portraitists, abstract painters, like Mark Rothko, and a top collector – Jospeh Hirshhorn, who endowed a museum and sculpture garden in Washington.

The tradition of Latvian painting dates back to the court of the Duke of Courland in the eighteenth century. Portraits of Ernest Johann painted by Caravaque and of his son Peter and his daughter-in-law Dorothea with children are by the artist Friedrich Barisian. Other prominent painters followed down the centuries including Eggink, Döring, Grass, Bertins, Roze, Feders and Alksnis until you reach Janis Rozentals (1866-1916) who is considered to be the founder of Latvian painting. Son of a blacksmith, Rozentals was a member of Rukis which included other talented people such as Vilhelm Purvitis who became internationally known because of his impressionistic canvases and Arturs Baumanis. The **State Museum of Art** has examples of their works and it is impressive to get this long historical perspective.

Another group of artists called the French circle rebelled against the Soviet regime through their Francophilia in the 1950s. One member Kurts Fridrihsons, was sent to Siberia while another in the 1960s, Imants Lancmanis was ordered to restore Rundale. The palace had deteriorated badly and had been used partly as a grain store and a boarding school. The splendid renovation was the making of Lancmanis as he achieved the impossible.

Painting has always been a strong suit of the country compared to the surrounding countries, Lithuania where sculpture has prevailed, and Estonia which has been foremost in high-tech cool intellectual forms of expressions like architecture and video installations. As a result, it has produced one of the world's top abstract artists Mark Rothko who was born in Daugapils.

Latvia's top ten artists

According to art guru Janis Borgs, the top ten are mostly painters. Ilmars Blumbergs who is also responsible for original opera sets; Ieva Iltnere (admirer of US artist Schnabel) Franceska Kirke, Janis Mitrevics, Helena Heinrihsone; Dace Liela, Boris Berzins, Inta Ruka (photographer and former cleaning lady at the Swedish Embassy and Venice Biennale 1999), Ojars Petersons (Professor of Art Academy, fan of Damien Hirst – 'a rare artist who knows what he's doing' and Venice Biennale 1999) and Anita Zabilevska (Video installations and Venice Biennale 1999).

There are some outsiders, like the abstract artist Madara Gulbis, the constructivist Peteris Sidars whose choice of materials can vary from sponges to peat and sloughed snakeskins and Edmunds Lucis whose subjects and technique remind one of a latterday Lucian Freud. His studio is located in a basement in the Old town at Klostera Street and is open to the public on certain days.

There is quite a buzz in the art scene and collectors are snapping up old and new canvases. Ieva Iltnere and Helena Heinrihsone have exhibited in Mimi Fertz in New York and the Zimery Art Museum in New Jersey. The latter is also a prize winner of the Air Baltic competition and her paintings are displayed on board their aircraft.

Ieva Iltnere

Ieva Iltnere lives in the fashionable quarter of the Right Bank, Kalku Street, in a large photographic studio. The living room, which has a view of the promenades below, is half the size of the studio at the back, where we stand and look at her latest painting on the easel, a double portrait of a woman with tears. The light streams in on this autumn evening not from south-facing windows but from a glass roof. Mounted paintings are stacked against one wall, with their canvas backs towards us.

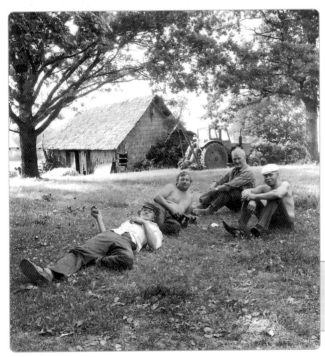

A photograph by Inta Ruka from the collection 'My Country People'

She was inspired by Man Ray's famous photograph of eight tears on a woman's face. A photograph is a significant element in her work, particularly when it captures an emotional moment which is transposed into a painting. Two versions of the tearful woman, a blue and white sketch and another in violet form the latest work. 'Without emotions no one will find your work interesting' she said in reference to this tearful theme, which reminded me of Kiki Smith's Mother, in which a cast of glass feet is mounted above some thirty large glass tears. 'The human factor always works. Why hasn't painting died out? Because it is unique, created by human hand and seen with human eyes'.

One of the articulate artists in Latvia, she has pondered the *fin de siècle* and with frankness expressed her apprehension.

'I got the feeling that as we approach the millennium' she explained, 'everything is happening at an accelerated pace. I can envision it as water flowing out of a bath. When it is full you don't even notice it, but towards the end the vortex spins faster and faster. We are now at the stage when the bath is almost empty. Purely visually now I'm frightened by the number 2000.'

'There is something I don't like about it – until I get used to it. Something new and unknown awaits. But in reality probably nothing special will change. So much has changed already, if we look back since 1991 (the date of Latvia's independence from the Soviet Union). It's a relative thing, but life has become more merciless'.

Anita Zabilevska

Anita Zabilevska, who is one of the younger generation, has tried another path. After the usual training at Rozentals' School of Art and the Academy of Arts, she studied philosophy of art and architecture at the Central European University, Prague. This equipped her with a wide approach to her subject and she combines the use of a variety of media such as video, installations and paintings for her work with a job first in architecture and now as an art director in an advertising company. This suits her personality as she is a loner, not part of the artistic clique and needs to explore the wider world to develop as an artist.

'I try to think of art from different angles' she said when we met over coffee. 'I hate the attitude of the typical artist who believes it is better to die than to think differently about art. They are so precious'. She enjoys working in advertising as it is a big part of contemporary culture and enables her to get at its core. How it works. She also found her period in architecture most inspiring. 'I'm like a hedgehog' she said, 'I collect impressions from all sources and perspectives which causes me to change my views constantly'.

She has exhibited in various European cities including Riga, Vilnius, Malmo, Warsaw, Lisbon, Wisby. Her recent one-man show in Stockholm used simple effects as she observed, 'I arrived in Sweden without anything in my suitcase'. It was an installation that required the public to stand in a square patch of light, in a darkened exhibition space and they would be reflected on screen in an unusual way. At first everyone wanted to escape but once a child ran into the light and produced the desired effect most people got the idea and joined in.

Art Collectors

The top entrepreneur, Valerijs Kargins has all the paintings of K Rosens and exclusively collects works by artists up to World War II, while Victor Krasovitsky is awash with L L Lieberts, a Maurice Utrillo figure who painted scenes mostly from postcards. Top bankers such as Dr Kari Nars, Director of the European Bank of Reconstruction and Development are assembling collections of Latvian abstract artists.

Modern painters are also in demand and can be found in galleries like Agija Suna, Bastejs. Daugava Noah (a floating non-profit art gallery near the Radisson

SAS hotel), M6 Art Gallery and Rigas. The Volmar art and antiques shop has a unique collection of over 1,000 canvasses of a forgotten artist, Adolf Zardinsh whose work was found some thirty years after his death.

'It is a miracle' said Janis Borgs 'similar to the discovery of a new island in the Baltic. His paintings have been described as Chagall-like and they look good in electric light as they were usually painted in a windowless room.

Right: A painting by Edmunds Lucis
Below: A video installation by
Anita Zabilevska

The Latvian Photographic Museum

MUSEUMS IN RIGA

Riga Motor Museum

When I heard that the only motor museum in the former Soviet Union was in Riga, the Latvian capital, I was not surprised. Russia's first car factory, the Russo-Baltic, was built there in 1909. I expected to find the Riga Motor Museum car collection housed in a Stalinist mausoleum. Instead, the building resembled a modern car showroom with a huge radiator grille as its façade.

Victors Kulbergs, founder of the Antique Automobile Club, initiated the idea in 1986. The goal was to collect and restore veteran, vintage and classic cars, motorcycles and bicycles. Today the museum's many exhibits are displayed on two floors above restoration workshops

Edvins Liepins, the current director, added another category to the collection – racing cars. But the museum's other outstanding feature consists of the vehicles of former Soviet leaders bought for a pittance from the Kremlin garage. Stalin, Khrushchev, and Brezhnev are represented by their 'wheels', and lifelike wax models.

Stalin sits at the back of his protected 1949 ZIS 115, his boots on his foot-rest, protected by three inch thick windows and steel plates all round. When each door was closed he drew a chain across to lock it like the security in hotel rooms. The car sports a chrome grille, three headlights, one in the middle of the radiator, a radio aerial above the windscreen and a Soviet insignia on the bonnet – a red flash with a silver star. Although very heavy, its 182 horse-power tuned engine made it the fastest car at the time. 'When the car was exhibited in Germany,' said Liepins, 'I had to share my room with Stalin's wax head. It was an eerie experience as he looked so real I could even see the freckles on his face.'

Brezhnev, who liked collecting and driving fast cars, sits in his 1965 Rolls-Royce Silver Shadow, a gift from President Richard Nixon. The car has been retained with the damage it suffered in a collision with a mammoth truck. The former Soviet leader – and his elegant machine – emerged almost unscathed from the accident. There were a couple of cracks in the passenger window and a slightly bent steering wheel. The front end took the greatest impact and the engine appears under the crushed bonnet.

A waxwork Krushchev stands next to a 1965 ZIL with its four headlights, panorama windscreen and V8 engines. To complete this political collection is the trophy car, the 1937 Rolls-Royce with an aluminium body, captured from the Germans during World War II and presented by Stalin to Molotov.

'The only car that is missing from this amazing collection is Lenin's Rolls-Royce,' says Tom Krooswijk, vice-president of Intercontinental Hotels. 'In this early model the two Rs of the insignia are red and not black. It's in his museum in Moscow.'

Another trophy car that the Soviet army brought back during the war was King Carol II of Romania's 1937 Special Packard Super with French Franay coachwork and a Detroit chassis.

Quality restoration is carried out on site and the low working costs have attracted business from collectors as well as car manufacturers' museums, including Audi's. The Russian cars in the collection include the tall ZIL (which incidentally is translated from Russian as 'named after Ligachov', one of the directors of the car company). Besides the 1980 Gaz, there are cars from the 1950s, the Moskvic, the Volga Gaz, the Pobeda (Victory) and the Gaz 12 ZIM, which is derived from a Cadillac design. In terms of the sophistication of their engines and the speed they could achieve, these machines were about twenty years behind equivalent cars built in the West.

German cars are another strength of the collection and include the only veteran car, a 1914 Hansa. This is a two-seater with exposed suspension and two carbide headlamps. The gas generating block for the lights is on the left running board, while on the right you find the reserve petrol tank and 'hunting horn' hooter. The steering wires are also exposed and resemble a child's go-kart design, connected only to the right-hand wheel.

Mercedes Benz, BMW, Horch and Opel cars are represented in the collection. The 1937 290 Mercedes has a comfortable interior and a good view of the road. It was fitted with a 12-volt electro system. The 68 horsepower engine had a top speed of 65mph (103kph).

The BMW 328, built a couple of years later, was even more efficient in terms of its powerful performance. Its 80 brake horsepower engine produced speeds up to 90mph (145kph). It is one of only 462 to be built.

For devotees of the classic Karmann Ghia marque, which made such an impact with its hardtop coupé design in the 1960s, the 1938 Adler two-litre EV will be of great interest. The upper part of this sleek and uncommon car is produced by the company, while the chassis and engine are from the Adler works.

There are four good examples of Horchs, three from 1939 and one from 1936, an 853. Of these, two are coupés and the saloon, an 830, is for sale at $100,000. This could be a bargain as the museum values its 1936 model at $200,000 or more. Both the Horchs and an open-top 1939 Opel Admiral with the body made in the famous Glaser Coachworks, are from the private collection of one of the top classic car owners, Egils Martinsone.

One of the most attractive cars in the collection is the 1938 Steyr 220 from Austria, which has an almost perfect aerodynamic body. With its 55 horsepower, six-cylinder engine, it could successfully compete against the larger BMW 327 with an 80 horsepower engine.

Among American cars in the collection is a 1929 De Soto, a 1934 Lincoln owned by the Russian writer Maxim Gorky and a beautifully restored red 1930 Ford A roadster. There are oddities such as a 1949 Tatra with a fin design from Czechoslovakia and the 1965 NSU Spider with Wankel engine.

Stalin's armoured car in the Riga Motor Museum

Open-air Ethnographic Museum

Open-air museums are not a well-liked venue but the Ethnographic Museum is more like a natural theme park. At weekends the visitor can see farmers, weavers, carpenters, blacksmiths, beekeepers and potters at work and at the same time get an idea of the traditional ways of life between the sixteenth and nineteenth centuries. There are reconstructions of old and ancient buildings from the four regions of the country and a taste is also given of the various regional fashions as participants dress in folk costumes.

The museum was founded in 1924 and the site chosen is ideal as it is placed in a pine forest alongside Lake Jugla which is a typical habitat in the country. The first building was an eighteenth century threshing barn and now there are over 120 buildings, of which the oldest is a sixteenth century wooden church that is hand painted inside in natural tones. The door is of particular interest, as it resembles a sergeant's V-strips shown in red rather than gold.

As visitors wander around the 247-acre (100-hectare) site, they will find organic forms. One thatched family home even had a special wheel on the roof for storks to nest. It was sunk low into the ground and had the largest thatched roof I have ever seen. Again wooden buildings predominate including windmills, there are beehives made out of hollowed-out trunks mounted on stones and farming implements. There is also an example of old wooden sauna

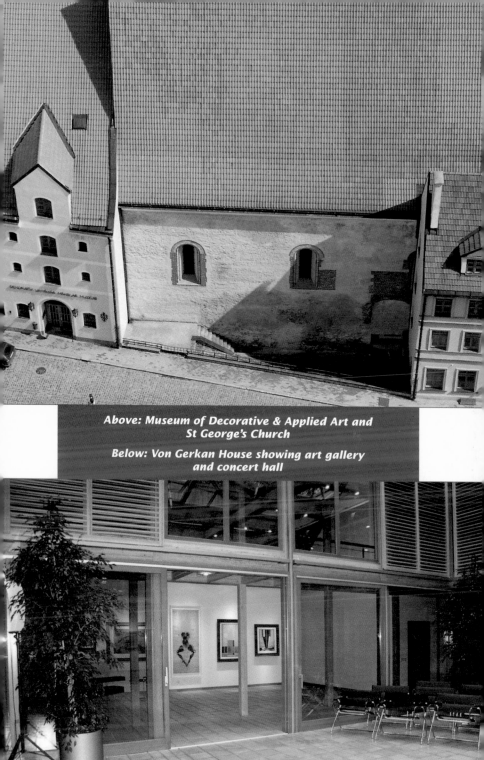

Above: Museum of Decorative & Applied Art and St George's Church

Below: Von Gerkan House showing art gallery and concert hall

which has been used since time immemorial by the Latvians as a maternity ward – it is warm and hygienic. In summer you can swim in the lake and in winter skate on the surface. If you are short of time to make an excursion outside Riga, this will do well as a substitute. It is a popular venue for Ligo.

The Jewish Museum

The link between Latvia and the Jews began as early as the fifteenth century when Jews were permitted to come to Riga on business for limited periods and were permitted to stay in special inns called 'Judenherberge'.

The Jewish Museum or Holocaust Centre, was founded by a group headed by the historian, Marger Vestermanis, who was a former prisoner in the Riga ghetto and the Kaiserwald concentration camp. Housed in two rooms on the third floor, it is principally a photographic exhibition and 'a memorial of the world that perished forever in torments and suffering' according to the curator, Lia Gherman. But there are also relics from different periods from the last world war. There is a huge framed Nazi map which shows the Baltic countries with the words 'Judenfrei' (Free of Jews) printed across them. To substantiate this statement a symbol of coffins is used with numbers of the Jews killed alongside in each country. A video of a film, made by a Nazi soldier, of an ethnic cleansing action can be seen on request.

There are also fine examples of how ordinary Latvians helped to save Jews at the expense of their own lives. Venerated are Zanis Lipke, Elvira Rone, Arturs Motmillers, Anna-Alma Polis and Andrejs Graubins. Some 150 Jews were saved and of the five rescuers, two – Anna-Alma Polis and Andrejs Graubins, perished.

A pamphlet, *Fragments of the Jewish History of Riga* includes a walking tour, with scholarly notes, of eighty-five sites and covers over three and a half centuries.

There is a thread running through the museum that demonstrates the significant role Jews had in Latvian society and the contribution they made in the arts, sports, political and intellectual life. Sir Isaiah Berlin who was born there is mentioned but not Mark Rothko which is an oversight.

State Museum of Art

The building was designed by Vilhelms Neimans, who was also the State Museum of Art's first director, and was built in the early 1900s to house collections from the Riga Art Museum and the Art Advancement Society. The influence of the Art Nouveau can be seen in the interior, particularly the banisters. It is the main repository of Latvian art from the eighteenth century to 1945 and has over 14,000 works including paintings, sketches and drawings.

The impetus for national art came from the second director, Vilhelmus Purvitis, the well-known landscape artist. The first floor contains Baltic and Russian paintings, including those of Nicolai Rerih, from the eighteenth to mid-nineteenth centuries. The second floor covers a chronological perspective of Latvian art from the mid-nineteenth century to the end of World War II. The ground floor has a mixture of Latvian and Russian portraits and landscapes. Of note is the portrait of singer Malvine Vignere-Grimberga by Janis Rozentals (1916).

J Rozentals and R Blaumanis Memorial Museum

Janis Rozentals (1866-1916), a graduate of St Petersburg Academy of Arts, and Latvia's most famous painter lived in what is now the **J Rozentals and R Blaumanis Memorial Museum** for eleven years from 1904-1915 before he escaped with his wife to Helsinki. He and his wife, a Finnish singer, had an artistic salon at the address. Rudolfs Blaumanis, a playwright, rented a room there for two years from 1906-8. Although Rozentals painted some 300 works, a small oeuvre is on show as well as photographs.

The Museum of Decorative and Applied Art

A visit is worthwhile, as there are two features of interest: the Museum of Decorative and Applied Art with exhibits of splendid porcelain, tapestries and woodcuts and the building itself which is the oldest stone building in the city. St George's Church, built early in 1200 and cited in the Livonian Indrikis Chronicle of 1209, was the chapel of The Knights of the Sword's first Riga Castle called Witgenstein because of the hue of the white stone. It ceased to be a place of worship during the Reformation when Catholic buildings were destroyed and was rebuilt in 1689 when it was used as a warehouse.

There are three exhibition spaces and the curator, Ilze Martinsone, has used them well. The first floor (where church services were once held) is used for new shows. On the second and third floors are permanent collections of applied art from the nineteenth to the twentieth century. Work of the most prominent artists of the 1920s and 1930s, such as the erotic art of Sigismunds Vidbergs, and interior décor of Ansis Cirulis are on show on the second floor. Examples from the porcelain painting studio called Baltars can also be seen. Of note is an Art Deco wedding plate designed by Romans Suta in 1928, and a superb sculpture titled *The Swimmer* by Stefans Bercs.

Museum of Foreign Art

The Museum of Foreign Art is a great surprise for it is housed in Riga Castle in halls with thirteenth century vaulted ceilings. It originated when the City of Riga was given Nikolaus Himsel's collection of paintings in 1773. He was a physician and art collector. There is an eclectic collection, from Ancient Egypt and Greece to paintings of Belgian artists of the 1930s. Some galleries are provocative as sculptures and curios from the ancient world are mixed with modern examples. Most European artists from England, the Netherlands and Germany during the sixteenth to twentieth centuries are represented, including drawings by Rembrandt and Goya. The key seems to be variety and minor rather than major works. Frieda Kahlo, the Mexican painter, is also represented as well as ceramics, glass, bronze, china and textiles. It also has a unique Meissen porcelain collection.

Arsenals Art Museum

The building housing the Arsenals Art Museum was designed by two St Petersburg architects, Lukini and Nellinger, in 1832 and was constructed to serve as a customs storehouse. It is a good example of classical style and offers a large selection of Latvian and European paintings, sculpture and decorative art. Of note is Fanis Pauluk's (1906-1984) portrait of Felicita with Sunshade.

Museum of History of Riga and Navigation

The Museum of History of Riga and Navigation has fine examples of Art Nouveau furniture, china, glass and applied arts. Of particular interest are birch chairs veneered with mahogany, a Kusnetsow ceramic dessert dish, glass vases from the local Ilguciems factory and picture frames.

Opposite top: A poster advertising the Song Festival of 1938

Opposite bottom: Fine example of Art Nouveau furniture at Museum of History of Riga & Navigation

Below: Interior St George's Church, part of exhibition floor of Museum of Decorative & Applied Art

History Museum of Latvia

This is a good museum run by Professor Arnis Radins. He has a wealth of material, some 600,000 objects, from the Stone Age to the present. It is interesting that the Latvians originated from four tribes, the Livonians, Semigallians, the Latgellians and the Selonians, and inhabited the Baltic together with the Baltic-Finnish people, the Estonians and Livs. Their territory spread east as far as Moscow. The Slavs only appeared on the scene as late as 700AD.

Latvian Photography Museum

The permanent exhibition of the Latvian Photography Museum illustrates the development of photography in Latvia from 1839 to 1941. There are early examples of historic processes like daguerreotypes, and cameras including the smallest camera in the world (1930s), the VEF-Minox which would have been standard equipment for spies. Photography exhibitions are mounted monthly.

Occupation Museum of Latvia

Last but not least is the museum is dedicated to the Nazi and Soviet occupation of Latvia.

Museum of Latvian Culture

The museum is of dual interest as the house in which it is displayed was owned by a brewer, A Bringners, and has been restored and is worth seeing. A collection of items reflecting Latvian culture is exhibited. It was also the residence of President Karlis Ulmanis.

• OPENING TIMES

ART GALLERIES

Agija Suna
6 Laipu Street and 9/11
Kaleju Street
Open 11am-6pm, closed
Sunday. ☎ 722 9529 and
☎ 708 7543 respectively.

Artist Union of Latvia
11 Novembra Kr
Open 11am-5pm, closed
Sunday & Monday.
☎ 722 8997

Bastejs
12 Basteja Boulevard
Open 12-6pm Monday to
Friday, 12-4pm Saturday,
closed Sunday.
☎ 722 5050

Daugava
7 Jana Yard
Open 10am-6pm, closed
Sunday.
☎ 721 2896

Noah
A B Dambis opposite
Radisson SAS Hotel
Ring to check exhibitions
and opening times.
☎ 947 0103

**M6 Art Academy
Gallery**
6 Marstalu Street
Open 12-11pm daily.
☎ 721 2640

Riga's
20 Aspazijas Boulevard
Open 12-7pm, closed
Sunday.
☎ 722 5887

Volmar
(art and antiques)
6 Skunu Street
Permanent exhibition
of Adolf Zardinsh.
Open 10am-7pm.
☎ 721 4278

**Janis Borgs Special
Dada Art Tours**
☎ 940 4009

MUSEUMS

Riga Motor Museum
6 Eizensteina Street
Open 10am-6pm
Tuesday to Sunday,
closed Monday.
☎ 253 7730

**Open-air Ethnographic
Museum**
440 Brivibas Street
Open 10am-5pm daily.
☎ 799 3306

The Jewish Museum
6 Skolas Street
Open 12-5pm Monday to
Friday, closed weekends.
☎/Fax 728 3484

State Museum of Art
10a K Valdemara Street
Open 11am-5pm,
closed Tuesday.
☎ 732 5021

**J Rozentals and
R Blaumanis
Memorial Museum**
12 Alberta Street
(the entrance is in
Strelnieku Street)
Open 11am-5pm
Monday, Tuesday and
Sunday, 12-7pm Friday
and Saturday, closed
Tuesday and Wednesday.
☎ 733 1641

**The Museum of
Decorative and
Applied Art**
10–20 Skarnu Street
Open 10am-5pm every
day except Monday.
☎ 722 2235/7833

Museum of Foreign Art
3 Pils Square
Open 11am-5pm,
closed Monday.
☎ 722 6467

Arsenals Art Museum
1 Torna Street
Open 11am-5pm, closed
Monday.
☎ 721 3695

**Museum of History of
Riga and Navigation**
4 Palata Street
Open 11am-5pm
Wednesday to Sunday,
closed Monday and
Tuesday. ☎ 721 2051

**Latvian Photography
Museum**
8 Marstalu Street
(entrance from Alksnaja
Street)
Open 1-7pm Wednesday
& Thursday, 11am-5pm
Friday, 11am-3pm
Saturday, closed Sunday,
Monday and Tuesday.
☎ 722 7231

**Museum of
Latvian Culture**
30 Sarkandaugavas
Street
Open 11am-5pm, closed
Tuesday.
☎ 739 2229

**History Museum
of Latvia**
3 Pils Square, Riga Castle
Open 11am-5pm, closed
Monday and Tuesday.
☎ 722 3004

**The Occupation
Museum of Latvia**
1 Strelnieku Square
Open 11am-5pm daily.
☎ 721 2715

RUNDALE PALACE

The Rundale Palace rivals Louis XIV's Versailles and you can find interesting echoes of the Sun King's motifs throughout.

Outside in the cobble-stoned courtyard, horses and carriages drove over a design of the sun with rays while the formal gardens were laid out with wide paths radiating towards the park. Inside, the Duke's bedroom is placed in the middle of the main buildings giving dominant views over the gardens and courtyard, enabling him to spy on the comings and goings. The bedroom is decorated with a sun symbol on the ceiling. Another solar feature is the interspersion of round windows in the attic of the quadrangular building.

History of Rundale

The Baroque and Rococo masterpiece belies a story of love, intrigue and power. It begins with Anna Ivanova, the daughter of Peter the Great's imbecilic brother, who was married off by her uncle at the age of seventeen to the Duke of Courland, Frederick William.

On the way back from St Petersburg to Jelgava (then known as Mitau), the Duke died and Tsar Peter ordered his reluctant niece to take over the government with the Russian president, Count Peter Bestuzhev, as her advisor. This was the original motive as it gave the Tsar an opportunity to gain a foothold in the Polish Kingdom. For a brief period, she was the Count's mistress before she met the love of her life, Ernst Johann Biron (or Bürhren) who also became a lifelong friend and counsellor.

Visit details

Rundale Palace, Pilsrundale, LV-3921, Latvia

Highlights

- Excellent example of Rastrelli's work which is on a par with the Winter Palace and Versailles, albeit on a smaller scale
- Superb renovated halls and rooms
- Original wooden staircase
- Only just over an hour's drive from Riga

If you need a royal recommendation, Queen Margrethe of Denmark has said it is 'One of the most beautiful palaces in Europe'

Open daily from 10am to 6pm from May to October, and from 10am to 5pm from November to April ☎ 396 2197, Fax 396 2274. The halls are available for functions such as weddings and birthdays. You can book meals in the restaurant for lunch and dinner ☎ 396 2116, or mobile 922 7369.

Ernst Biron

He was an ambitious adventurer who was expelled from Konigsberg University for riotous conduct before setting out to seek his fortune in Russia. But having failed he returned to Jelgava where he met Anna through his sister, who was also the mistress of Bestuzhev. He was three years older, and the grandson of a groom on the estate. He later married Benigna von Trotta-Treiten, one of her ladies-in-waiting and they had three children.

After the death of Peter the Great in 1730, Anna Ivanova was invited to return to Russia as Empress. On her acceptance of the Russian crown, she was forced by the supreme privy council to subscribe to nine articles that reduced her powers as a monarch. She bided her time and on 8 March, in a *coup d'état,* overthrew the council and was hailed an autocrat. Biron joined her in Moscow and she showered him with riches and veneration at her coronation in May. He was appointed Grand Chamberlain, given the title of count and an estate with an income of 50,000 crowns a year.

He became the all-powerful adored-one, and in keeping with the position, adopted the French ducal house of Biron and ruled the country in her name. Her government, through his outrageous insolence particularly towards the Russian nobility, was universally unpopular. Contemporary diplomatic sources depict him as mean, treacherous, vindictive and rapacious, and half the bribes intended for the court ended up in his coffers.

When the Winter Palace was completed as a main residence for the Empress he asked her if the renowned architect Bartholomew Rastrelli could build him a summer palace in south Latvia. She agreed and as he had acquired the bankrupt Rundale Estate, Rastrelli was dispatched to the site. It was a tremendous task but Biron was fortunate in the choice of the architect. He had extraordinary organisational skills and was one of the most energetic and talented men of his time.

Construction statistics

In 1735 over 1,000 craftsmen, as well as Russian soldiers, were involved in the construction. The mammoth scale of the operations was reflected in the calculation that to transport some three million bricks, 12,000 logs, 16,000 lime barrels and other materials, some 433 wagon loads were needed daily.

The foundation stone was laid in the same year 1736, when Anna Ivanova's Winter Palace was completed and this enabled Rastrelli to focus entirely on Rundale. Designs are still to be seen today as they are lodged in the drawing repository of the Albertina in Vienna. Rastrelli was as busy as ever, he even designed the coat of arms, but an event occurred which luckily would bestow two Rastrelli residences in Latvia and provide the master architect with another vast project.

The old childless Duke of Courland, Ferdinand, died in June

1737 and with him apparently the Kettlers dynasty. Biron saw the opportunity to succeed to the title and obtained the support of the Polish King August III. He also needed to be elected by Courland's nobility and managed to overcome their objections through the payment of large sums smuggled into the country in the form of bills payable in Amsterdam. Work was immediately begun on the main residence, a palace in the capital Jelgava on a site next to the River Lielupe.

Jelgava is 19 miles (30km) northwest of Rundale and Rastrelli was like a horseman riding astride two horses. The foundation stone of the new 300 room Baroque Palace was laid in June 1738. Although exterior work at Rundale was slowed down, the interior was unaffected. Reports on the progress of both buildings were regularly sent every fortnight to the Duke Biron.

Within two years the fortunes of Duke Biron changed dramatically. The Empress died on 28th October 1740. During her last days she ensured that Duke Biron would remain in a powerful position by appointing him regent to the baby Tsarevich Ivan. The son of her niece, Anna Leopoldovna he became Ivan VI against the superior claims of her cousin Tsarevna Elizabeth. According to a contemporary, Lady Rondeau, whose husband Sir Claudius was the British Ambassador at her court, the Empress was a grim, sullen woman and openly sensual. She was a true friend as indeed is shown by her treatment of the Duke, and in her cheerful moments, an amiable companion.

Biron's Exile

The duke's regency was short-lived. Three weeks later he was seized in his bedroom at midnight by a rival, Field Marshall Münnich. This was Tsarevna Elizabeth's revenge. Early the next year, when he came to trial and was condemned to death by quartering, the sentence was commuted to exile at Pelym in Siberia. All his property was confiscated including his diamonds, which alone were worth £600,000. Almost twenty-two years later, he was pardoned by Peter III, but it was Catherine the Great, who restored him to his former position in Courland.

Rastrelli returned to continue his work of reconstruction of both palaces. Rundale was completed in the mid-1760s and the palace at Jelgava in 1772. Duke Biron abdicated in 1769 in preference of his son Peter, and died three years later in the Jelgava Palace, where his body is interred in a copper sarcophagus. Only recently, it was discovered that Ernest Biron was the illegitimate son of the last Kettler, who had an affair with his mother Katharina.

When Catherine the Great annexed Courland, she gave Rundale to Count Valerian Zubov and later it was passed on to his brother, Prince Platon Zubov. After his death in 1822 his widow married Count Schuvalov and their descendants held it until 1920.

(cont'd on page 106)

The Gold Hall, most luxurious room in the palace

The house of Courland still exists and Prince Ernst Johann, who was born in 1940, is the current head and lives in Munich.

Tour of Rundale

The approach to the magnificent palace is over the canal bridge and through the semi-circular stables which were designed by both Rastrelli and the Duke's court architect, Severin Jensen. His distinctive trademark, maroon, was applied to most of his buildings although thankfully this is not the case with the gates with their lions, which he also designed.

For some reason the director has maintained fine sand underfoot in the courtyard, so it is preferable to wear sneakers rather than fine footwear on your visit, but this irritant is soon forgotten when you step up wooden stairs into the palace. Inside it is magical and the grand staircase takes you up to the Duke's living quarters and staterooms if you turn left, or to the Duchess' suite and dining room if you turn right.

Out of the 138 rooms, 42 are beautifully restored with period furniture and to the original interiors. Unlike other public buildings, you are allowed behind the scenes to see staterooms in the process of being decorated. (This is a risky business because there are potential dangers on the uneven surfaces and visitors should exercise great care in these rooms.)

The ground floor has the palace kitchens, part of which is a restaurant and part houses the museum. There is a hodgepodge of over 700 exhibits on display in the museum including furniture, paintings, sculptures, textiles, porcelain, glass and bronze covering the Gothic to the Art Nouveau period. An unusual item is a silver goblet owned by Peter, the Duke of Courland, which is inlaid with coins of the mid-1700s.

The pièce de résistance in the palace is found on the upper galleries. In the central building there is a series of rooms leading to the Duke's bedroom which contains two floor-to-ceiling stoves decorated in Delft blue tiles made in Danzig by the potter, Gottried Kater. The twenty interconnecting rooms run in parallel enfilades with a library at one end and a billiard room at the other. The Duke's private chambers run to two studies, a dressing room and bathing room.

The east wing contains the various reception rooms such as the Gold or Throne Room which is the most luxuriously decorated room in the palace with gilt stucco on artificial marble and has definite echoes of the War and Peace saloon at Versailles, and the Gold Gallery of Charlottenburg in Berlin. A surprising feature is the delicate Porcelain Cabinet.

The Grand Gallery, which served as the courtiers' meeting place, links the Gold Hall to the White Hall where balls were held and are still today, as it can be hired for special events. The latter can be described as a paean to whiteness, and it does not take much imagination to see how the resplendent ballgowns stood out as the women dancers swirled by. It also has a porcelain cabinet attached in an oval shape and the vases and jars are arranged to resemble a cascade of water. If anything, these rooms are a living celebration to the great talents of the Prussian sculptor Graff and the Italian painters Francesco Martini and Carlo Zucchi.

The Duchess' apartments in the west wing are simpler and smaller than the Duke's. An outstanding feature is the divan niche in the form of an enormous shell, designed by Graff, in her boudoir.

Around Rundale

The nearest town is **Bauska** which is worth a visit because of its castle and can be reached by car in an hour or hour and a half by a regular bus service from Riga. I suggest you combine this with a visit to the Neo-Classic **Mezotne**

Manor House, owned by the von Lieven and situated a short distance away. It has a brilliant rotunda and is open daily from 9am to 5pm, ☎ 392 8921 or 392 8796, Fax 392 8984. A descendant of the family who lived there until 1920 is Anatol Lieven, Russian Correspondent of the Times.

Rastrelli fans may consider a visit to the **Jelgava Palace**, which houses the tombs of the Dukes of Courland. The Baroque building is a shadow of its former glory and is now run by the Latvian University of Agriculture. The Jensen maroon dominates brightly against the white outside. Some twenty-one sarcophagi rest in the crypt including Ernst Johann and his father Duke Ferdinand. Open Monday to Friday 10am to 5pm, ☎ 302 5329.

NORTH OF RIGA

Hieronymous, Karl Friedrich, Baron von Munchausen (1720-97) of Bodenwerder in Hanover had served in the Russian army against the Turks and when he retired to his estates around Dunte, he would amuse himself and his cronies by relating extraordinary stories of his deeds as a soldier and hunter. He became famous in literary history because of his amusing, mendacious, anecdotes, known as *The Adventures of Baron Munchausen*.

An author, Rudolf Erich Raspe, down on his luck in London, and who had met the Baron, collected them in a shilling book of forty-nine pages which was published in London in 1785. No copy of the book, known as *Baron Munchausen's Narrative of his*

Marvellous Travels and Campaigns in Russia, exists but a second edition was printed in Oxford in 1786. A bookseller named Kearsley, brought out an enlarged edition later that year with illustrations under the title of *Gulliver Revived: the Singular Travels, Campaigns, Voyages and Sporting Adventures of Baron Munchausen*; as he relates them over a bottle when surrounded by his friends.

There were seven English editions as Munchausen increased in popularity and the book was translated into many languages. A sequel appeared in 1792, dedicated to James Bruce, an African explorer whose book, *Travels to Discover The Nile*, was held to

(cont'd on page 110)

Above: The Red Study next to the Duke's bedroom

Right: Exhibits in the Palace Museum

Below: The Araisi Lake Fortress

ridicule and incredulity. In time, additions were made by bookseller's hacks and suggestions were taken from Baron Toff's Memoirs, the aeronautical feats of Montgolfier and any topical subject such as Bruce's explorations in Africa.

Munchausen, as we know it, is a medley of material from all ages, from Lucian's Vera Historia and Renaissance Facetiae to contemporary travels, real and imaginary.

The country house in Dunte is no longer there but an old pond where he caught five ducks at once with a piece of bacon tied to a thread can be seen. The Munchausen Museum is sparse on exhibits and includes two pairs of old hunting boots, the aforesaid stuffed ducks strung across the ceiling, animal trophies on the wall and a sled.

Although the Baron is out of fashion today his name has been used to describe a bogus medical condition, Munchausen Syndrome. The patient simulates different medical conditions on a regular basis to gain attention even to the extent of undergoing surgical operations. This can also occur when a parent makes a child ill or pretends they are ill and requests medical attention, Munchausen's Syndrome by proxy. Such a situation can happen often and the child recovers when separated from the parent.

The most interesting place is the pub next to the museum which has good traditional Latvian cuisine and is open every day from 10am

• PLACES TO VISIT •

Munchausen Museum
Dunte Vidzeme
7.5 miles (12km) north of Saulkrasti
Open 10am to 6pm Wednesday to Sunday. Closed Monday/Tuesday. ☎ (40) 20333, (40) 20107

Bicycle Museum
44a Riga Street, Saulkrasti
You can also take in a bicycle museum with thirty restored machines including a Dutch penny-farthing.

Cepli ceramic workshop
Before the Dunte-1 sign on the right off the Riga-Tallinn road. A selection of milk pitchers, vases, mugs and bowls are on sale and the kiln is in the potter's backyard. Ingrida Zagata has been casting pottery for the past fifteen years.
☎ 923 4867

Araisi Lake Fortress
Cesis Region, Drabesis, LV-4140. Open 10am to 6pm, May 1 to October 15. ☎ 419 7288/7293

to 9pm. There are bonuses to visiting his museum. There are the wild beaches of Saulkrasti (sunny shore in Latvian) where you can swim and which can vary from sand with high dunes and stony beaches to meadow beaches where grass grows to the water's edge.

The Araisi Lake Fortress

A window to the past life of Latvia's largest tribe the Latgallians during the late Iron Age (ninth to tenth century BC) is shown at a castle built on a sandbank in the middle of the lake. There was a local legend of a fortress, the **Araisi lake fortress**, sunk in the lake and it was only in 1965-1969 when archaeological excavations were carried out that this was found to be true. The dig was difficult as the water level had to be lowered 3ft (1m) and dykes had to be built around the excavation trenches. Nevertheless, water seeped through and had to be pumped out.

Several interesting aspects were revealed about the Latgallians. An archaic form of house construction was used unlike any other found in building. These were single log cabins with sloping roofs, covered with strips of spruce or birch bark inside rather than ceilings and an annexe, the sleeping quarters, was attached to the right of the entrance. The door frames were rather low indicating short people who also had to be agile to walk on the round surfaces of the log platforms.

Each house had a clay floor with benches along the walls. There were ovens and shelves for cooking utensils and sculptural figures of the inhabitants dressed in their clothes. Necklaces, bracelets and remnants of clothes were found as well as ancient tools, like narrow bladed axes, chisels and wooden wedges, with which the buildings are being reconstructed.

The whole complex of over twenty houses was surrounded by high walls and the archaeologists were surprised to discover that the island was not a natural formation but purpose-built.

The concept of a fortress surrounded by water is not new, as a similar arrangement was still in existence in the sixteenth century in Mexico City. The Aztec capital during Montezuma II's time, which was on a grand scale compared to Araisi, was built on a lake and could only be reached by a causeway which had a series of bridges to allow sea traffic past.

The Conquistadors had to fight hard to conquer the city, as it was well protected by the surrounding water and only one causeway which could easily be defended. There were also fleets of canoes which could bring in supplies in the case of a siege and attack anyone who appeared on the causeway. The Latgallians would have had a similar stronghold in the middle of the lake when attacked by the Vikings. In a country which has some 4,000 lakes, water fortresses would have been popular and could have provided adequate protection from enemies and wild animals.

The Araisi lake fortress is the only Iron Age site in Latvia and the first in north-east Europe to be extensively studied. There are other attractions, a fourteenth-century church and castle which is in ruins.

Culture

One of the greatest ballet dancers of the 20th century, Mikhail Baryshnikov

THE LITERARY SCENE

Little is known about Latvian literature as few works have been translated into English and on my visits I was fortunate to meet a poet and two authors. Like other states under Soviet occupation, a systematic attempt was made to eradicate their culture. But this was not a new situation as it had occurred before under other rulers and champions have always risen among the people to defend their heritage.

When the German Barons had sneered at the peasant lifestyle in nineteenth century Krisjanis Barons rose to the challenge and produced his encyclopaedia of Dainas, a six-volume collection of songs. (See entry, Dainas). In the last century, Janis Rainis, issued a figurative call to arms and defend the Latvian identity with the publication in 1905 of the verse collection *Vetras Seja (Seeding of The Storm)*. But this was a subtle force, without violence or bloodshed, that swept the country stimulating a new thinking and consciousness.

Mara Zalite, editor and publisher at *Karogs* magazine, was another figure from the literary establishment to voice her concerns at a meeting in the Riga Philharmonic Auditorium to commemorate those who died during the Stalinist purges. 'We have been made to feel like exiles in our homeland. We have been expelled from our spiritual birthplace. Banished from our way of life, driven from our farmlands. Torn away from our culture – severed from our folklore!

Separated from our songs – cast out of our language! Driven from Europe – exiled from civilisation!'

She was unaware at that time that freedom was only a stone's throw away, for a year later independence was declared again, the second occasion in the twentieth century.

I was met at the Salapils station by Knuts Skujenieks, one of the country's foremost poets and translators. We walked for half a mile (1km) along a dusty and broken pavement, towards his house in a quiet cul-de-sac, where I was going to spend a night.

Once I had settled into my room, Knuts and his wife, Inta, a botanist who cultivates their large vegetable garden at the back of their house, welcomed me with a drink of vodka and a meal. 'It is a special' he said of the vodka. 'I bought it as it comes from Jelgava, the town where your father was born'. I was touched.

Knuts was proud to show me his study, which was a light and compact room at the top of an

Knuts Skujenieks

Knuts Skujenieks is sixty-one years old and soon after graduating from the Gorky Institute of Literature in 1961 he was sentenced to seven years in camps for telling political anecdotes. 'There is a strange notion, that to mature as a creative person", he said, "you have to suffer. I do not subscribe to that concept. I saw the time in prison as only a small period of my life unlike other prisoners for whom it was the peak of their existence. I got out of the camp alive and relatively unscathed. What followed for them was a plunge into non-existence'.

He published poems he wrote behind barbed wire in a collection, *Sekla Sniega (Seed in the Snow)* in 1990. 'When I read other people's memoirs about deportations and Gulag, I am deeply humiliated because it is terrible to be deprived of one's freedom'.

open staircase. The shelves were chock-full with his translated works from over thirty languages and several volumes of his poetry.

Our conversation was wide ranging from eighteenth century history to Dainas and analysis of Latvia's psyche. He told me about the Lutheran clergyman Ernst Glück who lived in Aluksne and made the first translation of the Bible into Latvian. When the town was captured by the Russians in 1702, he and his family, including his child's nurse Marta Skrovronska, a Lithuanian, were taken prisoner. It was this selfsame woman who became Catherine I. Taken to St Petersburg she first became the mistress of Prince Menshchikov a friend of Tsar Peter the Great and, then the Tsar's consort and wife. Another interesting fact about Aluksne, which I learnt later, is that the author of *The Leopard*, Guiseppe de Lampedusa, lived there in the Manor House in the 1930s.

For him, the Dainas are marvels because in only four lines there are unlimited possibilities of expression. The perfect square of two lines about nature and two about human life allows this. His most preferred is the one about the godfather, which is a symbol of the sun.

'Dear Godfather
what will you do
  when all of us die?
Who will give you the
  bread in your old age?'

Before we part the next day, I ask him about the Latvian society since Independence. 'There are many hang-ups' he said 'We are masters of our destiny yet we still think with a slave's mentality. We lack initiative to solve problems and still think we will find the answers through an executive body. There are still many who suffer from self-pity. They complain we're small, we've been oppressed and are dying out as a nation.

When I returned to Riga I knew I had been with a sage because however many questions I asked him, he was always ready to give me a considered, incisive opinion.

During our discussion on Dainas, he immediately suggested that I meet the world authority, Dr Vaira Vike-Freiberga, and he rang her up so I could make an appointment to see her. I did and within a month, I heard she had been elected president. Later, I found that the mention of his name to others was equivalent to a letter of introduction.

Andrea Neiburga is quite different. She considers herself as being part of the second generation of writers, the first was under the Soviets who always toed the line, for them criticism meant ostracism, exile and possible death. When I was told about her brilliant collection of short stories and expressed an interest in meeting her, the secretary of the Writer's Union suggested I make an appointment through her secretary. I was impressed as I thought she had landed a fat advance and begun a spending splurge because she is one of the few Latvian authors whose work has been published in English.

As we sat in Osiris, one of the in-places in Riga, she disabused me of my notions. She had stopped writing since independence and the secretary that has been referred to, helped her run the family's real estate business. This is a loss, as she was particularly well known for her satirical style. She wrote of the annihilation of the human ego felt during the collapse of the Soviet Empire.

'My generation was very shocking about reality' she said 'and there were a lot of opportunities to sell stories. Now it is hard to make a living from writing. That's why I am in business'. She points to others from the third generation, Paul Bankovskis whose most well-liked author is Roddy Doyle and Janis Einfields, originator of the super-short story. They are in the vanguard of experimental writing. The others have fallen silent. There is little now to challenge and no government line to espouse. Social realism is dead.

The Writer's Union has also fallen on hard times. They formerly occupied a mansion belonging to the Benjamin family situated in the middle of the city, and when it was recently returned to the owners, the Union moved to small, new premises out in the suburbs. Knuts Skujenieks welcomes this new era. 'I prefer the dirty, tiring prose of every day life' he said after he had won another of his innumerable awards. 'The fact that we can tramp around the base of the Freedom monument, yelling and screaming, or say what we think of our president... ha! ha!'

Now that is something to write about but first the latter day Philip Roths or John Updikes must get under the skin of the cult of individualism.

Collections of Latvian writers in English include:
1. *New Latvian Fiction, The Review of Contemporary Fiction*. Ed. John O'Brien. Illinois State 1998.
2. *World Literature Today, The Baltic Literatures in the 1990s*, Vol. 72, 2 Spring 1998.
3. Neiburga, Andra. *Mosy Death – Description of a struggle*. From the *Picador Book of East European Prose*.
4. Neiburga, Andra. *Stuffed Birds and Caged Birds*. AGNI 33, Boston University.

• Pushkin's Love in Riga •

In the churchyard of the former St Peter and St Paul Church which is now the Ave Sol concert hall, there is an unusual monument, a sculpture of the head of an attractive woman, Anna Kern, who inspired Russia's greatest poet.

She was born in 1800 in the Orel province where her grand-father, I P Wolf, was the Governor. But her parents moved to Tversk, 93 miles (150km) north-west of Moscow where she grew up. At the age of sixteen she was married off against her will to a fifty-two year-old, General Ermolay Kern, who had impressed her parents with the prospect of making a good match.

As a couple they were a total disaster as he was a professional soldier, having been promoted through the ranks and caring only about the army. She had artistic aspirations, had read widely during her youth and acted in amateur theatricals. Her husband was coarse and she abhorred him. She lived the life of an army wife, moving from town to town and bore him two daughters. Life was tiresome as her husband was either asleep, on army duties or smoking. She complained that she had 'not a single soul to talk to' and her head spun from all the reading.

A notable event in these early years was a meeting with Tsar Alexander during manoeuvres in Riga in 1817. He found her attractive and invited her to visit him in St Petersburg. She declined, but asked the Tsar to come to Lubny, where they were stationed. He laughed off her suggestion.

In 1824, when she returned to her parent's estate, she was given copies of Pushkin's poems, along with the first chapter of *Eugene Onegin*, by Arkady Rodzyanko who lived next door.

On another visit from Riga a year later, this time to her aunt, Praskovya Alexandrovna Osipov-Wolf, she met the poet who had been exiled to his father's estate, Mikhailovskoe, because of his involvement with the Decembrists. He appeared during lunch carrying a tall stout stick, which, according to Anna Petrovna, was his usual habit. He usually ate earlier and would be accompanied on his visit by two large wolfhounds.

When he was introduced to her, he said nothing. He tended to avoid the people living in the vacinity who became butts of his satire in *Eugene Onegin*. However, the Osipov-Wolfs who lived at Trigorskoe were an exception as he enjoyed their company and large library. Unpredictable in his manner, he showed a full range of emotions when he was there from noisy exuberance, bouts of depression, shyness and sadness.

'Incapable of hiding his feelings', Anna Petrovna said, 'he always expressed them sincerely and was indescribably good when something pleasant excited him. When he decided to be friendly, nothing could compare with the sparkle, the wit and attractiveness of his speech.'

They saw each other daily and the night before she left her aunt suggested that they paid a visit to Mikhailovskoe. They set off in two carriages: Pushkin, Anna Petrovna and her cousin Anna Wolf were in one and her aunt and son, Alexey Wolf, in another. 'Never before or afterwards did I see him so kind and cheerful' she remarked. 'He joked without sarcasm and sharpness, praising the moon without calling it stupid.'

They did not go into the wooden house, which Pushkin called his hut or izba, but went to the old, overgrown park. There they walked down an avenue of lime trees and he recalled their meeting six years earlier before he left St Petersburg. But seeing her again had rekindled tender feelings and inspired one of his finest love poems, *I Remember the Wondrous Moment*.

The next day before she set off for Riga with her cousin, Pushkin arrived with a copy of chapter two of *Eugene Onegin*. He had also written a poem for her and hidden it in one of the uncut pages. It was the love poem:

'I remember the wondrous moment
You stood before me
Like a radiant fleeting dream
A vision of perfect beauty'

And after four verses it concluded:

'Once again my heart is filled with elation
It's excited and delighted
and awake to inspiration
Awake to life, love and tears'

She read it and when she wanted to place it in her casket, he had second thoughts and snatched it back. Later she repeated the lines to his great friend Baron Anton Delvig who printed them in his magazine, *Northern Flowers* and to Glinka who set them to music.

Pushkin was in the throes of a crush on her and wrote to her cousin in Latvia. He told Anna Wolf 'every night I roam the park and repeat to myself "she was here". The stone on which she stumbled lies on my desk, beside a branch of fading heliotrope'. Another missive was also sent off to the aunt. But the longing for her became hard to bear and soon, on 25th July, he wrote directly to her asking whether she would agree to correspond with him, and happily she did.

'A correspondence leads to nothing, I know; but I do not have the strength to resist the desire to have a word from your pretty

(cont'd overleaf)

• Pushkin's Love in Riga •

(cont'd from previous page)

hand', he writes frankly. Then he struck a Byronic pose in the second part of the letter. 'I take up my pen again because I am dying of boredom and I can't get you off my mind'. Next he sensed the danger of an affair with a married woman which excited him. 'I hope you will read this letter in secret... will you hide it again in your bosom? If you fear my indiscretion... Sign with a fictitious name, my heart will be able to recognise you'. One can imagine Anna Petrovna walking along Citadel Street, Riga and smiling to herself about the affair, her secret secure in her bosom.

The family was housed in the officer's quarters adjacent to the Barracks in the square. Sometimes, she may have entered St Peter and St Paul Church and lit a candle for the Almighty to bless their love.

Pushkin had been exiled by Tsar Alexander I for six years and he would have chafed at the thought that he could not go to Riga when his romance with Anna Petrovna turned into passionate love. His mother wrote an emotional letter to the Tsar on his behalf requesting permission for him to travel to Riga to consult a specialist there, purportedly for his varicose veins. It was refused.

She returned in October to Trigorskoe with her husband and the lovers managed to be alone several times. They discussed plans for her to separate from her husband and hints of this appeared in one of his letters to her. 'This is the fine project which has plagued my imagination for the last quarter of an hour. Yet imagine what would be my happiness. You will say: "But the explosion, the scandal?" What the devil! Upon leaving a husband the scandal is complete, the rest is of no consequence'.

After her short visit, he referred to her in another missive as 'an angel fate sends to delight my solitude'. When he later discovered that she had been also corresponding with Alexey, in a fit of pique and jealousy he dismissed her as 'our whore of Babylon' in a letter written to him later.

A year later she left her husband and went to live with her father in St Petersburg in the same house as Delvig. On some occasions she carried out errands for Pushkin, who was still confined to Mikhailovskoe, and once sent him a book of Byron's that he had requested. Not much of their correspondence survived from that period except a letter which she had written jointly with her cousin, Anna Wolf. 'Anna Petrovna Kern orders me to tell you that she is selflessly delighted by your success... and loves you sincerely, with guile'.

She was present on his nameday in 1827 which was celebrated with his family. When a friend remarked that she had not given him a gift in return for his poems, she took off her mother's ring and put it on his finger. He promised to match her gesture and the next day gave her a ring with three diamonds.

There is always the question of whether their love was ever consummated. Evidence is provided in a reply to a letter from a friend 'Falstaff' Sokolevsky, who worked in the Department of Foreign Affairs. 'You don't write me anything about the 2,100 roubles I owe you!' he wrote, 'but you write me about Mme Kern, whom with God's help a few days ago I fucked'.

There were other amours after Anna Petrovna until he married Natalya Ivanovna Goncharova. Incidently another Tsar, Nicholas I, took a fancy to her and it is likely that she succumbed to his charms. The Tsar later made provision for her and the children after Pushkin's death.

The woman who came from Riga was the one he immortalized as a vision of perfect beauty. In the Pushkin museum in St Petersburg, there is a copy of the poem that she transcribed, as well as a good imitation of his signature which she signed for her scrapbook. She is buried on a small estate, Mitino, in the family graveyard some six versts (4 miles/6.4km) from Torzok. There is also a Pushkin museum in the old trading town dedicated to his travels in the Tver region where he had stayed with his many friends on their small country estates. Strangely enough he had done sketches of the park and the graveyard too.

Although Pushkin never managed to see Riga, there are strong associations with the city because the descendants of his closest friend, Delvig, originated from the city and of Anna's presence there.

Dainas – songs

Like the ancient Greeks, Latvians have a strong oral tradition, but theirs has not been in epics like Homer's *Odyssey* and *Iliad* which originally were sung, but in folk songs. They focus on nature, on the panoply of Gods, on human relationships, on the seasons and life, and earlier ones on the Sun like the Ancient Egyptians. Essentially, they are philosophical and have provided wisdom for the Latvians over thousands of years.

It is as unique to the Latvians as *haiku* is to the Japanese. The first two lines of the quatrain present an image from nature, the last ones echo with a parallel from human life.

An example:

'The meadow is beautiful
but it is most beautiful when it
is ploughed
A bride's wreath is beautiful
But most beautiful is a married
woman's hat'

The Dainas were classified according to several major themes. One cycle followed the stages of human life from the cradle to the grave with the attendant family feasts and rituals of which weddings were most numerous. A second followed the solar year with seasonal festivals and celebrations, mid-summer songs being the most popular. A third significant category is devoted to work songs while a fourth is about singing itself. In addition there are mythological magic spells, children's, and erotic songs.

The Academy of Sciences in Riga has logged over three million songs, which is the largest collection in the world. An assiduous compiler, Krisjanis Barons, who was a mathematician and astronomer, published six volumes of almost 182,000 song texts between 1894 and 1915 at the time when the country was run by the German minority and ruled by Russia. A nationalist, he had been provoked by the German Barons who intimated that the Latvians could not have a culture as they were peasants. The encyclopaedia of Dainas was his answer. The task took him three decades and was begun by meticulously filing bits of paper in shoeboxes and later transferring them into seventy drawers of specific size to contain them in a special custom built cabinet.

Dr Vaira Vike-Freiberga, the President of Latvia, is the world's leading authority and exponent of the Latvian Dainas. For her each of the songs represents a poem. 'They are implosions of creativity within the confines of strict metric frameworks' she says. 'On the surface the Dainas speak of apparently mundane, concrete things; yet the concrete is but a vehicle for a deeper abstract idea. The Dainas do not depict concrete reality, they transfigure it. It is the verbal alchemy that takes the common metal of all that the singer encounters and transmutes it into poetic gold.'

The recorded song texts are a pale shadow of what a song would have been when it was sung. 'Live' songs accompanied by a melody occur in a specific social context. They are aimed at an audience, be it a baby in a cradle, a festive crowd such as a wedding, Midsummer Night celebration (Jani) or the singer themselves while they are grinding grain on a handmill.

According to Dr Freiburga this largest single repository of published and oral folklore is a rich seam of the ancient Latvian way of life revealing the daily tasks, cares, joys, sorrow, beliefs, customs and values of the people. There are echoes of an old cosmogony, a mythology and a social order, and they take on a breadth and scope that acquires an epic quality.

Without a doubt this oral tradition of songs serves as a cultural history of the Latvians. But some claim it is more for it has gathered and documented a people's way of life, their philosophy, moral code and aesthetic judgement and as such should be considered to be like the Old Testament.

Latvians are indebted to Barons who has returned their unique heritage to them through constructing a vast verbal monument. It is the first time in the history of mankind that an unbroken cultural record exists of a nation over thousands of years. The fact that it is still relevant today demonstrates its flexibility and resilience. As such, it should be looked upon as a gift to the West, which is on a par with anything that the Greeks or the Romans gave, but unlike the Latvians, they have vanished.

The final word should be given to Dr Freiberga who puts the Dainas into their present context. 'The Dainas allow us to reconstruct a metaphysics in which the highest aim of a human life is to live in harmony with the will of the gods, with the rhythms of nature, and with other members of society' she says. 'Personal worth and integrity are expressed in terms of possessing virtue, not in terms of avoiding sin, which is a concept alien to the Dainas. The basis of personal virtue rests on reverence for the gods, respect for one's elders, and the indefatigable ability to work hard all one's life.'

This sounds like a perfect viewpoint for the twenty-first century.

Since 1873, traditional song festivals have been held every five years. The last festival occurred in 1998 and took place in Mezaparks. Some 20,000 singers and dancers participated over a week.

The President, Vaira Vike-Freiberga, a world expert on Dainas

• A detailed look at the Dainas •

The first song in the enormous collection of Krisjanis Barons was:

> 'One girls sings in Riga
> Another sings in Valmeira
> Both sing the same song.
> Could they be daughters of the same mother?'

Most of the songs are quatrains and their lyrical quality derives from the fact that they are never objective descriptions presented by a detached narrator. They are live testimonials from active participants cast in the first person of the lyrical 'I'. The singers are often transposed into the roles suggested by the lyrics. Take the following examples:

> 'Why, o sun, did you tarry
> Why did you not rise earlier?
> I was delayed behind the hill
> Warming the little orphans'

A third couplet can be added:

> 'I warmed hands, feet
> I dried off their tears.
> The swan swims
> on the river.
> I swim
> among other people's gossip'

A simple interpretation of the swan's song is that a girl's reputation is sullied through gossip and her repartee is that as water does not cling to a swan's feathers, nor will the ill remarks of others cling to her.

The four-line strophe is the fundamental building block of the huge edifice of the folk song corpus.

The Dainas, mostly, do not refer to specific people like Lize or Milda or Mikus or Peteris. They are universal, referring to the eternal bride, mother, father, bridegroom, brothers, or sisters.

> 'A bright star came down
> By the door of my bride
> That was not a bright star
> That was new born child's soul'

The major periods of human life are marked off through successive rites of passage including marriage, funeral rights and the comings and goings of the seasons.

> 'Black ravens are crouching
> At my graves edge
> These were not black ravens
> Relatives stand crying'

Like other cultures, there are examples for the archetypal mother-in-law, who is a pain in the butt.

'Not every morning the sun rises
With red little rays
Not every day my mother-in-law
Was good to me'

Or

'I heard in the kitchen lean-to
Fir logs spluttering
That was not fir wood
That was the son's mother'

Trees in the Latvian language have association with the different sexes. Thus ozols (oak), osis (ash), vitols (willow) and berzs (birch) are male, while liepa (linden), ieva (bird cherry tree) and abele (apple tree) represent the female. The Latvian abele is a word of ancient Indo-European origin since the stem is known in at least three Baltic languages.

There are further distinctions with tree types as an apple tree is motherly, a linden is a young girl and a bird cherry tree is frequently a wife or a bride. The oak on the other hand, represents three kinds of males; boys, men or husbands.

The fourth volume of Barons' Dainas contains an entire section about woods and trees and 20 different kinds are mentioned. Apple is the fruit of love according to the linguist Velta Ruke-Dravina and 'is easily discerned in the erotic songs of the sixth volume of Latvian Dainas where a woman's breasts as well as male genitals are compared with apples.

In sexual songs the motif about 'driving the little horse through the apple grove' has the same meaning as 'I gave the rose garden to the little horse to harrow'. There are associations too with the Greek myths where the apple is also a symbol of love and fertility.

Of special interest to Dr Freiberga, is the cycle of Sun songs of which there are some 4,500 texts. Sun or Saule (pronounced sowleh in Latvian) is a feminine noun and appears in songs as a beautiful female figure. It is the mythological and divine being that is being conjured up. When an orphan girl marries, the sun a generous godmother enriches her plain wool cloak with gold shining floss.

A significant task of the setting sun is to bring along with her the souls of all those mortals who have been laid to rest in the earth on the preceding day.

'My dear mother has left
Along with the sun
I called out, but she couldn't hear
I ran after her but in vain'

There is the lovely physical aspect as the sun is the celestial timepiece, with its sunrises and sunsets and in the heralding of the seasons. This is framed in the Dainas, but again repeatedly, one finds the philosophical:

(cont'd overleaf)

(cont'd from previous page)

> 'What shall I earn
> While living in this sun?
> Two sheets of white linen
> A room of four planks'

Or as Goddess or God-like figure

> 'Dear White Saule in your course
> Please 'even out' this earth
> The rich are quite ready
> To bury the poor alive'

The Latvian pantheon is filled with divine personages to rival the Greeks, the Romans or the ancient Egyptians. Laima is a version of Athena for she can take a human form and appear amongst people. She determines the fate of mortals as is shown:

> 'As Laima cast my life
> So must I live it
> I cannot go counter
> To dear Laimas decree'

Or

> 'Rise early, my Laima dear
> Be late in retiring
> Help me to lighten
> My life's heavy burdens'

Mara, who is looked upon today as Mother Latvia, is closely linked to cows. She is invoked during childbirth and like her counterpart in Egyptian mythology, Hathor, she is a mother of heaven. Janis, which means the Johns, has a dual role echoing the two-faced Roman God. He is the force of attraction between male and female and also plays the Dionysian role during the midsummer night feast. The equivalent of Jupiter in this heavenly firmament is Dievs, which originates from the Indo-European word, 'The bright Sky'.

> 'Higher sings the lark
> Than any other bird
> Dievs holds wise council
> Over the whole of the world'

One of the aspects of virtue; tikums' is to respect Dievs, to 'hold' him as the Dainas put it. This does not mean humbling oneself before him or them. When someone suffers ill fortune, or is oppressed, the Dievs or Laima will 'lift them up' and restore their self-respect.

Tikums consists of several desirable character traits. A lack of virtue is not cause for a feeling of guilt but for shame and the price is ridicule and ostracism.

BALLET

Riga School has had its fair share of top ballet dancers such as Maris Liepa and his son Andris, John Markovsky and Vladimir Gilvan but it has also produced one of the greatest stars this century – Mikhail Baryshnikov. The school is situated opposite the old town across the river in the suburb of Pardaugava although in a new building. His teacher, Juris Kapralis is still on the staff coaching future stars.

Mikhail Baryshnikov was born in Riga in 1948 after his father, Nikolas, an Air Force officer was sent to the city as a lecturer in military topography. It was a second marriage for both parents and his mother Alexandra brought along Vladimir his stepbrother who was eight years old. Mikhail had little in common with his father, a cold, curt man and more with his mother who was interested in culture. She would always take Misha along when she went to the theatre, opera or ballet.

As a boy Misha had 'ants in his pants' and could never sit still. When Alexandra became friends with a ballerina from the Bolshoi Ballet in Moscow who gave ballet lessons, she enrolled him in the classes. He was nine years old and she felt he could channel his energy into dance. It was a good decision as Misha had a talent for expressing himself in movement.

'I got lucky,' he said. 'I fell in love with dance'. Two years later he was accepted at the state ballet academy, the School of Choreography, and was put in Juris Kapralis's class together with Alexander Godunov who became

a friend. 'Even as a small boy he was very musical' said Kapralis, 'but he also had the huge possibility for hard work.'

An event occurred in Misha's life which although tragic gave him the impetus to develop his talent. He had gone on a visit to his grandmother who lived on the Volga river outside Gorky. For some reason his mother returned to Riga earlier. She hanged herself in the bathroom of the communal flat. She was found by Vladimir and his father was loath to talk to him about it. It was a traumatic experience as he admits he was 'mamma's boy'.

When his father got married a year later, Misha understood that he was no longer welcome and began to lead a peripatetic existence. He stayed with other families for periods and then the ballet school would ring them up and warn them that they should send Misha home otherwise they would have to call the police. He went through all the problems of teenagers and worried about his height. He believed he was too short to be a ballet dancer and slept on a wooden plank to grow faster. He was fortunate that

Teacher's recollections

'He was a perfectionist' Kapralis said 'and serious. When the class had free time, Misha would go into a corner and reherse over and over again'. But there are other qualities which a dancer must possess, besides a big talent. According to his teacher, 'You must be physically strong, a good actor, an excellent partner who provides stability and strength, be good at jumps and turns, and above all, have a good technique'. He gives the example of the *Nutcracker*. 'Misha, who played the toy soldier, would always think of his role. I was dancing as the prince, when the mouse king died, I noticed that Misha relaxed his body'. When he was asked why he had done this, he replied 'When Mouse King dies, toys become human. Toys become boys and must change'. I was impressed because even as a small boy he had devised that himself'.

Kapralis had a sunny disposition and was a brilliant teacher, so Misha thrived, not least because he was a child workaholic.

When Baryshnikov reflects on this difficult period he is not bitter. 'Human beings are extraordinarily powerful survivors' he said 'When you lose your parents it is a fact of life'. He was grateful though that his mother did not commit suicide in front of him. Although he never had a serious relationship with his father he does not blame him as he feels he is responsible for all the difficulties in his own life.

In 1964, the Latvian State Ballet went on a tour of St Petersburg and the teenager Baryshnikov went with the company in a small role. During the visit he met Alexander Pushkin, a teacher, at the Kirov Ballet School and was asked to join the class. Kapralis was proud of this and when he asked after Misha later he was told by the Russian, 'Please give me more pupils like Baryshnikov'. There are three great ballet dancers of the twentieth century according to Kapralis, Nijinsky, Nureyev and Baryshnikov.

'He was fortunate' said Kapralis, 'because he gained an intellectual approach to ballet from us as opposed to the Russian School which is strong on bravado and can at times be mannered. Here he learnt acting, good form and good line'.

Kapralis has a superb reputation for nurturing talent and one of his new stars is a twenty-one year-old Pavel Vasilchenko. He met Baryshnikov on his last visit to Riga two years ago and is still impressed with his former student. 'Now he dances in another way', he said, 'Modern dance is easiest when you are older. But he is still number one for his age'.

Mikhail Baryshnikov defected to the West in 1974 and is now living in the US directing an American modern dance company, the White Oak Dance Project. Alexander Godunov is a principal dancer in the company.

The Riga School of Choreography is at 10/12 Kalnciema Street, ☎ 761 5870.

MUSIC

'**M**usic is the most cultivated of the fine arts. A good operatic company, and five singing clubs are among the amusements of Riga', *The John Murray Handbook for Travellers in Russia, Poland and Finland,* 1865.

Music has been one of the oldest forms of culture as Latvian songs date back to time immemorial *(see entry Dainas)*. The songs gained recognition when the first song festival was held in 1873 and was followed by Krisjanis Barons' encyclopaedia of Dainas, which was completed in 1915.

Richard Wagner

Even before that, Riga was firmly established on the provincial music circuit and Richard Wagner was one of the first eminent musicians to have engagements in the city from 1837 to 1839. In fact he was desperate to come to the city 'I am breadless' he wrote to his friend Louis Schindelmeisser from his sister Ottilie's house in Dresden 'I must get Riga'.

When the director of the theatre, Karl von Holtei, offered him the post, he travelled by sea, which was cheaper than the land journey from Lubeck, at the end of August via Travemunde, where he had to wait for a week for an agreeable wind. He took lodgings a few minutes from the theatre in Schmiedestrasse and found that his qualifications for the job had been his supposed interest in light French and Italian music which was popular with the patrons.

However, the composer did not tell Holtei that he was undergoing a change of heart and had gained a dislike for such musical trivialities. His emotional problems with his wife Minna, he contemplated divorce, and his dire financial circumstances had no doubt contributed to this state. There were other sources of irritation; the stage, the orchestra, the theatre, the company which was incomplete and the small audiences, only 3,000 patrons out of a population of 70,000.

While he was in the city he managed to arrange a temporary position for his sister-in-law Amalie Planer a singer, and at the same time became reconciled with his wife Minna. She and Amalie arrived in Riga on 19th October 1837. Soon the trio moved to more spacious accommodation occupying the top of a house at the corner of Dzirnavu and Brivibas streets.

It was large and consisted of a salon with windows overlooking each street, a bedroom for the couple, two rooms for Amalie and Wagner's study with a divan, a hired grand piano and a desk on which he wrote the first two acts of *Rieuzi*. People living nearby remembered Wagner sitting at an open window smoking a pipe and dressed in a dressing gown with a Turkish fez on his head.

The composer Richard Wagner

Minna had made the ill-founded decision not to work, and they decided to live on Wagner's scant income. There was speculation that the decision was due to Wagner's jealousy. She flirted with the theatre patrons and there is a suggestion that she had an affair during her marriage.

He set about his task as musical director with energy, zeal and perfection, which was normal for his theatre work. Fifteen operas were rehearsed and produced during the first year and twenty-four in the second. He was an unforgiving taskmaster, a role that did not please the company, as nothing was good enough or finely shaded for him. There were endless rehearsals and soon complaints and grievances from the singers and members of the orchestra were commonplace.

Matters were not helped by the fact that Wagner was antisocial, he did not disguise his distaste for fun-loving, empty-headed audiences or the bland repertoire. A further offence was that he refused to write incidental music for the theatre director's mediocre plays. And he also set a new tradition for conductors, for he no longer faced the audience during a performance. He turned his back on them.

Although Minna was slightly ill when she arrived she was easy to live with because of her repentant attitude and her desire to please her husband. However, his peace was disturbed when Amalie was replaced by another singer, and in her disappointment began to quarrel with her sister. Soon they no longer spoke to each other.

It was a matter of time before Wagner was in debt and his financial position became known at the theatre. Although he was living on a knife-edge he was undergoing inner development which made him indifferent to his outside world. He had enemies at the theatre, no friends in the town and his one consolation was that his work on *Rienzi,* on which he had pinned his hopes for material success in Paris, was progressing well.

In a letter written to Theodor Apel after his departure of this period he said with a trace of irony; 'I obtained a good and respectable post as music director in Riga. There I spent two fairly tranquil years; I might almost say that there I began to feel myself again but for the fact that it became ever clearer to me that I am not built to earn my bread in this way. I sought stupefaction in the almost frenzied performance of my duties; but my body was not fitted for this, the northern climate being trying for me'.

By March 1839, the crunch had come, his unpopularity with the performers and overwhelming debts, which if payment was enforced by the creditors could land him in prison, forced the hand of the theatre committee and he was dismissed. As the dismissal only came into effect in the summer, they also laid plans for his flight from the city.

Wagner was furious when he was sacked and railed against Heinrich Dorn, a friend who had been appointed to replace him. 'I had a serious illness, a nervous fever threatened my very life. Hardly had I begun to recover when I heard that during my illness my seeming friend Dorn had displaced me in the most perfidious manner' he wrote to Apel in the same letter.

Wagner's room

To escape from Latvia which was part of Russia was no easy task because the frontier was well guarded and anyone proposing to leave the country had to advertise their intention in the local newspaper, in the event of creditors having a claim on them.

When the company went to Mitau, as Jelgava was then known, Wagner decided to leave the country there, where he was unknown. By arrangement he and Minna were smuggled over the border to Prussia as contraband goods by Polish Jews. Robber, a huge Newfoundland dog owned by a local Riga merchant, that had taken a liking to Wagner, accompanied them.

They were taken to Pillau in Prussia and not Konigsberg, which was nearer, because he was on the creditors wanted list there too. From there they sailed to Paris, the focal point of the operatic world, and to fame and fortune. He did not conquer Paris and had to wait another three years before *Rienzi* brought him that success he had hoped for in Dresden.

The Riga period, on hindsight, was seminal as he was inspired to begin a sketch of the *Flying Dutchman* on his voyage from Pillau. Because of stormy weather this had taken three weeks instead of eight days. Wagner had matured sufficiently to shed his illusions and develop his artistic ambitions that would result in the Ring.

He left his mark on the city too. Most of the opera audience at the time were unaware of his importance and were astonished at his later fame, but were generous enough to name the theatre after him as well as the street where it is located.

Musical visitors

Other musicians such as Anton Rubinstein, Robert Schumann and Klara Wieck, before she married Schumann, Franz Liszt, and Hector Berlioz followed in his wake and the tradition has continued into the twentieth century when Bruno Walter, Benjamin Britten, Otto Klemperer and Carlos Kleiber visited the city. Dimitri Shostakovich also found a haven here after he had fallen into disgrace with Stalin and his works were no longer performed. The opera, *Lady Macbeth of Mzensk* was premiered in Riga in 1946 and conducted by Edgars Tons.

After Wagner

The interesting question is whether anyone of Wagner's stature has emerged since. Jazeps Vitols (1865-1948), founder of the Latvian Academy of Music is considered one of the country's greatest composers. He was a teacher at the St Petersburg conservatory and friend of Nikolai Rimsky-Korsakov. Most of his contemporaries like Melngailis trained at St Petersburg as the new generation would study at the Latvian State Conservatoire of Music. The two main contenders for the slot of top composer appear to be Imants Kalnins and Peteris Vasks.

Straight away, I must mention that it is hard to make a living from composing classical music in Latvia, let alone anywhere else in the world, and that Imants Kalnins is also an MP. He had several brushes with the Soviet regime and their tough tactics, so that later when the country achieved independence, the exercise of political power appealed to him and he became a member of parliament.

He recalled an occasion when an official from the Union of Composers told him he could not perform a new oratorio *The Poet and the Mermaid.* The story is about a sea sprite and a poet who longs to follow her to a new world.

'I still remember the woman in the office, she was not belligerent or rude, she simply shook her head and said "No, we can't allow this to be performed". When asked why she smiled, "These two lives, they're too mystical, I can't quite understand these two lives". I asked her maybe you think it represents capitalist life and socialist life. She grinned at me "I don't know, but you can't perform it".'

'Everything was politics', he said 'Every word. Even your smile. It was jail, a real jail'.

His interests as a composer are wide and his oeuvre includes rock and pop music, a passion that began in the sixties when he toured with his rock band. He enjoyed star status and when a popular folk-rock band Menuets who performed Kalnins' compositions were banned he came to their aid. The oppression stopped when they added his name to their list of songwriters.

'But there's also this patriotic element to his music as well' said Imants Mezaraups of the Medins Music College in Riga who high-

lights his mass appeal, 'Its typical for Latvians to break out with folk songs in the middle of dinner parties, including Kalnins' songs'.

Indeed his work is closely identified with the symbol of resistance during Soviet times and his symphonic pop fourth symphony was performed on the seventy-ninth anniversary of Independence on 18th November 1997.

Peteris Vasks who was born in 1946 and is five years younger than Kalnins was never attracted to political power. On the contrary he has resisted politics with every fibre of his being. Of his work Cello Concerto, which was dedicated to the celist David Geringas and completed in 1994, he made a strong statement about his position.

'I wanted to tell in music of the persistence of a personality against crude brutal power', he said 'About sources of strength which helped us to endure it all. What totalitarian power did to us. How we are to purge ourselves from the manipulation. Above all, how we are to carry on with our lives'.

When he wrote the *Book* for solo cello in 1978 he was asked about the inclusion of the wordless human voice. 'An important factor in my music', he explained 'has always been spirituality and protest against power. I wrote mainly instrumental music, which did not come under KGB control. They could control literature and cinema but they could not understand instrumental music!'

In Latvia, he is considered to be a serious composer whose work is appreciated abroad. He is also not popular with the mainstream like Kalnins 'I write music not for the

(cont'd on page 134)

The gardens and canal next to the Opera House

New influences

Vasks was not allowed to study in Riga as Kalnins did, because his father was a Baptist minister and was forced instead to go to the nearby Lithuania's State Music Academy. The only Latvian composer of his generation to do so, he came under unusual influences like the avant-garde Polish music of Witold Lutoslawski, which made a memorable impression on him. He studied ancient music, classical drama and mastered technicalities of twentieth century works of Schoenberg, Webern and Berg.

Unlike Kalnins who won accolades under the Russian regime – winner of the All-Union Competition of Young Composers in 1969, State Prize winner in 1977 and Peoples Artist of the Latvia Socialist Soviet Republic in 1985 – Vasks abhorred political hack work.

He points out the positive aspects of that period. 'Under the Soviets, concerts meant more here as people listened attentively to the undercurrent of spiritual protest in the music' he said. 'This unified the musicians and the audience. Of course you don't want the iron curtain back, but in such an atmosphere music is very important to people'.

mass of people but for the individual' he stated firmly.

I was keen to know what the international music scene thought about him and talked to Yakov Kreizberg a young and brilliant conductor who was born in St Petersburg where he was a music prodigy, before he emigrated to the US when he was sixteen. He is an outspoken musician, who is chief conductor of the Komische Opera in Berlin and of the Bournemouth Symphony Orchestra, who persuaded the BBC to commission a piece from Vasks for the 1999 Promenade concert.

He was first introduced to Vasks through David Geringas who when they did a concert together played the music for his encore. 'It was stunningly beautiful' he said of the *Book* for cello 'That got me interested in Vasks. Later when I bought the first CD which featured the euphonious *Cantabile for Strings*,

I thought it was terrific and now the work is part of my standard repertoire.'

The *Book* had a similarly powerful effect on an indie label producer. John Kehoe who heard it on the car radio was to produce several CDs on Conifer.

Soon Kreizberg also wanted a new work from Vasks because of its reflection of the twentieth century and its conflicts. He wanted the composer to break out of his small world of the chamber orchestra. He did this with the Second Symphony which was premiered in the Royal Albert Hall, London and was Vasks' first large scale work. 'It was like a child who had a few toys to play with being let loose in the toyshop' was how Kreizberg described the experience.

If he was to place him in the music constellation, Kreizberg is adamant that he is a major figure whose works are deeply Russian

Russian heritage

When Kreizberg was asked whether he still considered himself Russian, he answered with great honesty 'My understanding of Russian music, literature and culture is in the blood'. He also explained how to play Shostakovich's music because the wrong tempo radical changes the effect.

'When I hear Shostakovich's music' he said, 'My bones ache' – it was the only way he could express his pain, his anger and contempt. 'I'm not saying non-Russians can't do it justice but they don't automatically know what lies behind it. 'If you play the first movement of the Fifteenth Symphony at a brisk tempo, as some do, it becomes perky, a parody, like a joke. If you play it slightly slower it becomes scary and menacing and that's the way I believe he meant it. It's the same with the finale of the Fifth Symphony. It doesn't take much to make a difference between it sounding triumphant or evil. That's typical of Shostakovich'.

in the richness and depth of the melody. There are certain gestures which you would find in Shostakovich for example. But then again the Second Symphony sounds very English because of the strong presence of nature besides the bird sounds.

'It's music of our time' he said 'The composer is committed to nature and deeply religious whether you believe in animism or God, and there are the brutal conflicts of the twentieth century reflected in it too'.

Andrejs Zagars

Andrejs Zagars, General Manager of the Latvian National Opera, is a latter-day Diaghalev and Balanchine all wrapped up in one. There is the impresario who wants to create fresh new productions quickly, and who wheels and deals with money and people. Then there is the artist who wants to nurture (audzinat) young talent, to train them and to push them to excel. Take for example *Eugene Onegin*, which I saw and discussed with him afterwards. It was first staged in Riga over a century ago in 1896 and was sung in German but this time it was in the original Russian.

For the stage director, Victurs Kairiss, it was only his third production and a risk to Zagars. 'I had to trust him' he says 'and usually I'm saved by my intuition'.

In this instance he is right. Kairiss succeeds in balancing the ironical man with 'a young woman with an open soul whose ideal is love... and then comes an arrogant... attractive male who possesses a strong masculine aura and demonic strength and provokes in Tatyana emotions incomprehensible to her'. Her possession is shown in wild bedroom scenes where she feverishly writes letters on the bed and sees his image on the mirror, which is used to brilliant affect as a projection screen.

Conductor Yakov Kreizberg

The other memorable scene is the duel, which occurs at a height on a narrow bridge.

The overall effect is not tired or stale but exciting. It is not unusual therefore that he is packing in the audiences and during his brief reign of about three years he has increased attendances from sixty-three per cent to an enviable eight-six per cent, figures that the current Chairman of Covent Garden would no doubt goggle at. Another amazing fact is that Zagars does this for the same amount as it takes to keep say Sir David Frost in Havana's a month – $300.

Unlike other artists before him, Nureyev and Baryshnikov, who dreamt of escaping to the West, there was no Margot Fonteyn or Gelsey Kirkland respectively, into whose arms he could fall. The big question in his mind was could he live in any other country than Latvia?

During Independence he decided to travel in Europe and the USA and live abroad. After two years in exile he believed he was too homesick and returned. He still acted in both films and the theatre, but decided to change his career. He became a restaurateur. 'In Soviet times, bars and restaurants were in dark cellars' he says 'as people didn't want to be seen and wanted to talk in secret.'

In 1993, he opened the Black and White Bar which was decorated in a minimalist, modern style that has now become his trademark. Six years later he is hailed as the Latvian 'Conran' with four restaurants, a bar and a wine shop. He goes by the dictum less is more and a visit to one of his places bears that out as you will find cool, clean, modernism reminiscent of Conran's Butlers Wharf.

It was his love of food and interior design that brought him back into the theatrical world of musical drama. 'My soul is happy when I'm running something and not being a slave of a bad director'.

There were many problems at the Riga Opera House and one day he got a call from the Prime Minister, Andris Skele. 'He told me that he wanted someone to kick ass and asked whether I was willing!' This was the way the offer was put to Zagars. The house had become

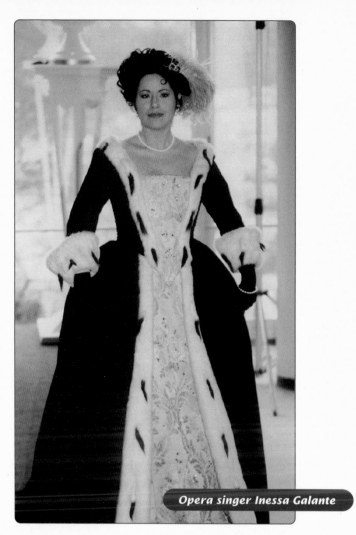

Opera singer Inessa Galante

a laughing stock amongst the Latvians, and a butt of jokes, as it was being managed by a wealthy timber merchant who had been brought in because of his business acumen. But he was no match for the Soviet style administration and he and the productions floundered like a fish on land.

Zagars had the right qualifications with the appropriate commercial experience, a creative background, and was ready for a challenge. He had new ideas that he was impatient to put in to

practice, and not afraid of taking on the old truculent establishment. The opera scene world-wide is known for its intransigence, particularly in the face of reform and many houses, like Paris have seen off potential saviours or creative Czars. The Latvian Company was no different and he immediately ran into a fight when he decided to join as General Manager.

He shrugs off those days with 'I'm used to being in stormy waters, but the difference was that I was not the Captain of a small

Andrejs Zagars' early life

Andrejs Zagars is without doubt a fascinating fellow. Before opera, he was a matinee idol in Soviet films. With his clear-cut handsome looks and non-Slovak features, he played foreigners and I wager that if he had been born in the West he might have ended up playing Superman or a Rambo-like character in Hollywood. He is over 6ft (1.8m) tall, fit and his personal dynamism makes him welcomed to any group.

He was born in Siberia of Latvian parents and when they returned to their homeland in 1959 he studied mathematics and physics. There was an inevitable draw to the theatre and movies and in his short film career, he has appeared in fifteen pictures. His main roles were playing heroes and he eventually tired of this, 'In my soul' he says 'I felt uncomfortable' The best film he acted in was *Good Luck Gentlemen*, which was directed by the famous Russian director, Bortko. This is the only one in which he does not win the girl in the end.

He was happier in the theatre and some of the productions he played in include Eugene O'Neils' *Long Days Journey into Night*, Shakespeare's *Romeo and Juliet* as Mercutio and Goldoni's *Servant of Two Masters*.

boat but a huge tanker which takes time to turn. I'm in charge of 610 employees, and responsible for everything'. His mission was clear. He would create the best singers and musicians, the best opera house in the Baltics and eventually in Europe.

Such talk did not appeal to some of the incumbents who were selfishly interested in maintaining the status quo, even if it meant blocking other younger and talented singers, musicians and dancers. The fight turned ugly and some members even resorted to voodoo, sticking pins into the costumes of their rivals. 'At times I felt I was in the trenches' he muses 'and the only loyal person I had was my assistant who joined with me'. In the end, there were three casualties and Zagars had won the war.

The climate was good – the artistic levels were high and he could build on the tradition of excellence. He was also inspired by the newly renovated Riga Opera House that was built in the 1860s. 'I wanted to ensure that the art here was worthy of such a magnificent building'.

Fulfilled mission

He was now able to carry out his mission statement of the best opera and gave major roles to talented young singers like Sonora Vaice and Inga Kalna. They have fulfilled his prediction of brilliance and have received acclaim in Austria and the United Kingdom. Placido Domingo raves about Sonora and has performed with her on many occasions. She has brought star quality to the title role of Handel's *Alcina*. Inga Kalna is another discovery who has found a perfect role as the Countess in Mozart's *Marriage of Figaro*. Another newcomer who has come out of the Zagars stable is the young conductor Andris Veismanis. Already, there are several Latvian international stars, the likes of Maris Janson, Inessa Galante, Egils Silins (Guesting at the Met) Gidon Kremer and Misha Maisky. The quality of the orchestra's strings is worth commenting on as it has produced the latter two stars.

Zagars does not bemoan the fact that he is not heavily financed like the eighty opera houses in Germany. 'When society gets state funding there is a tendency to become complacent' he observes. The productions are usually led by stars and produce boring performances in which there is no story, little acting and none of the components blend together. Such a situation, in his eyes, is wrong. 'Opera is a drug for me, not the stars. I want to make it a moving experience so by the end of the evening you are transformed. We achieve that once or twice a year, *Aida* is one example'.

Opera economics is blighted by the star system that results in high ticket prices which limits the audience to an elite. The people who come to the performances in Riga are a cross-section of the public and the prices are low in comparison to other houses. The General Manager's target is to get a full house on each occasion to ensure future interest in this art form. Educational programs are being developed to understand good art and the opera.

The LNO with its 1,100 seats is certainly worth a visit and the restaurant, which is situated under it and was once a resonator to contribute to its perfect acoustics, will not disappoint. Every year in June, there is a special festival and in 2000 from 7-18 June the following operas will be performed:

Romualds Kalsons —
The Prodigal Son
Wolfgang Amadeus Mozart —
Die ZauberFlöte
Gaetano Donizetti —
L'Elisir D'Amor
Pyotr Ilyich Tchaikovsky —
Eugene Onegin
Giacomo Puccini —
La Bohème.

Hotels

In general, hotels are expensive and often do not meet the usual standards of European and US hotels. As a result you are paying a lot for basic accommodation. There are a few exceptions and I have starred them. The main reason is that there are insufficient rooms in the city and as yet no major chains like Marriott, Intercontinental, Holiday Inn, Sheraton or Hilton have opened up hotels in the city or at the sea resort, Jurmala.

There is a big choice of accommodation from bed and breakfast in private homes for as little as £6 or $10, to youth hostels and former Intourist hotels; at the seaside of Jurmala there are apartments and hotels.

LUXURY

***** **Radisson – SAS Daugava**
361 rooms.
24 Kungu,
☎ 706 1111, Fax 7061100,
E-mail radisson@com.latnet.lv
Website www.radissonsas-riga.lv
The most luxurious and leading business hotel in the Baltics which is situated on the left bank with a brilliant view of Old Town across the river, excellent facilities include top restaurant The Grill Room, American Café, sauna, swimming pool, fitness suite and 10 air-conditioned conference rooms. Service is excellent and the beds the best in town. It offers free transfers from the airport and an hourly shuttle bus to the Old Town, which is within walking distance.

Park Hotel Ridzene
95 rooms.
1 Reimersa,
☎ 732 4433, Fax 728 2100
It is centrally situated between the Esplanade Park and canal area. A luxurious business

hotel which has just undergone renovations it offers a presidential suite, the Piramida Restaurant, Summer Café, relaxation complex with gym and sauna, facial and body treatments and conference rooms. The only pity is that you have to work up a sweat to see the superb view as the sauna and gym are located on the top floor and the restaurant is on the ground.

Hotel de Rome
90 rooms.
28 Kalku,
☎ 708 7600, Fax 708 7606
It is a shame that the hotel does not live up to its excellent location and good views of the city. The service is poor and the décor kitsch. The restaurant, Otto Schwarz, is over-rated.

Metropole
80 rooms.
36/38 Aspazijas Boulevard,
☎ 722 5411, Fax 721 6140,
E-mail metropole@brovi.lv
Situated at the unfashionable end

of the Old Town towards the station, it is the oldest hotel and in the 1930s was the focus of intrigue. The décor recalls the days of espionage and the best rooms become furnaces in the summer as there is no air-conditioning and the windows cannot be opened.

Man-Tess

6 rooms.
6 Teatra,
☎ 721 6056, Fax 782 1249
This miniature hotel is housed in an eighteenth century building and yet manages to have a restaurant and a banqueting room. The décor is slightly over the top and exotic.

Eurolink

59 rooms.
22 Aspazijas,
☎ 722 0531, Fax 721 6300,
E-mail eurolink@brovi.lv
Located on the third floor at the Riga Hotel, it has a 'smorgasborg' décor like the Metropole because the same management runs both hotels. Facilities include sauna, solarium and hairdressing salon.

Riga

243 rooms.
22 Aspazijas Boulevard,
☎ 721 6285, Fax 722 9828
It has one of the best locations in the Old Town, facing the opera. A former Intourist hotel, it retains some of their quaint traditions whereby slips of paper are given to you at check-in and these are exchanged for keys at a key desk on your floor. A vast cavernous place, it is in dire need of refurbishment.

MODERATE

*** Konventa Seta or Konventhof

140 apartments and rooms.
9/11 Kaleju,
☎ 708 7501, Fax 708 7506
Within the restored courtyards of 10 medieval buildings, it is one of the most picturesque locations in the city. It is a well-run hotel with conference rooms and a restaurant, Raibais Balodis. A quiet, pleasant ambience with friendly staff.

Laine Hotel

28 rooms.
11 Skolas,
☎ 728 9823, Fax 728 7658
It is situated in an Art Nouveau building in the New Town in a street with other notable buildings in that style at No.'s 3, 4 and 6. In a quiet courtyard, it is good value.

Radi un Draugi

49 rooms.
1 Marstalu,
☎ 722 0372, Fax 724 2239
Good location in the Old Town and is owned by British Latvians.

Latvija

55 Elizabetes,
☎ 721 1755, Fax 728 3595
Former Intourist hotel built during Soviet times, has a splendid view from its 26 stories. The quirks which Colin Thubron found on his stay during the 1980s and mentioned in his book *The Russians* still exist – scuttling sound of the electricity and leaks from the showerhead. It is still short on charm.

Tia
49 rooms.
63 Valdemara,
☎ 733 3918, Fax 783 0390
Comfortable and clean. Good
value for its central position.

Turists
210 rooms.
1 Slokas,
☎ 761 9090, Fax 786 0008
Situated a bit out of the way, on
the left bank near the largest
park, Uzvaras and the Under-
ground nightclub is next door.
Choice of rooms from singles to
renovated suites.

Mara
24 rooms.
186 Kalnciema,
☎ 790 1316, Fax 790 1315
A Best Western hotel on the
airport perimeter and near a golf
course. Quiet and clean.

Brigita
22 rooms.
11 Saulkalnes,
☎ 762 3000, Fax 762 3190
Preferred by businessmen for
long stays, it is located on the left
bank about 20 minutes by taxi
from the middle of the city. It has
a sauna, bar and café.

INEXPENSIVE

Valdemars
23 Valdemara,
☎ 733 4462, Fax 733 3001
This is a find as it is located in an
Art Nouveau building designed
by Scheel and Scheffel with some
original stained glass windows
and a splendid wrought-iron
door (see Art Nouveau tour).
Spacious singles and doubles.

Saulite
28 rooms.
12 Merkela,
☎ 722 4546, Fax 722 3629
One of the cheap hotels around
the station.

Arena
45 rooms.
5 Palasta, ☎ 722 8583
A popular place because of
position near the Dome. Communal showers and toilets.

Mezaparks
32 rooms.
19 Sakses,
☎ 755 7988, Fax 755 7964
On the outskirts of the city in the
expensive part of town with good
views of Lake Kisezers. Basic
clean rooms with tennis and
watersports facilities during
summer. End of the line for trolley
bus No.2.

Oskars
64 rooms.
9a Krusta Baznicas, ☎ 755 6955
Latvian Army Hotel near Lake
Kisezers with swimming pool,
sauna and gym. Simple but clean.

Latavio
At Riga International Airport,
☎ 720 7149
Simple accommodation.

Aurora
5 Marijas, ☎ 722 4479
Near the station with basic rooms
and communal showers and
toilets.

Bed and Breakfast

Riga Tourist Information
At Airport ☎ 720 7800,
              Fax 720 7100
City   ☎ 722 1731,
            Fax 722 7680
            E-mail tourinfo@lgs.lv

Patricia
22 Elizabetes, Apartment 6,
☎ 728 4868, Fax 728 6650,
E-mail
patricia@riga.mail.telia.com
Can also provide apartments for
long stays.

Hostels

Hostel Association
29 rooms.
2a Laimdotas, ☎ 755 1271

Riga Technical University Hostel
30 rooms.
22a Azenes, ☎ 708 7261
Communal bathrooms, toilet and
kitchen.

Turiba
50 rooms.
68 Grandu, ☎ 790 1471
Café, sauna and fitness complex.

ACCOMMODATION IN JURMALA

Jurmala, the seaside and spa resort of Riga is some 15 miles (24km)
from the middle of the city. Trains, buses and taxis provide a good
service into Riga and many visitors prefer to stay here during the hot
summer months.

Hotels

MODERATE

Rigas Licis
126 rooms.
Jaundubulti, 51 Dubulti Prospect,
☎ 776 1180, Fax 776 1166
A spa hotel situated in a pine
grove and 100yd (100m) from
the sandy beach. One of the best
hotels in terms of décor, sports
activities like tennis, full range of
spa treatments including mud,
thalassotherapy and medical
consultations. Modern building
with balconies, sea views and
conference facilities.

Rigas Jurmala
98 rooms.
Majori, 23-25 Juras,
☎ 776 2295, Fax 789 2705
Good location on the sandy
beach at the largest village.
Seawater swimming pool and
wide range of spa treatments,
thalassotherapy and medical
consultations. Seaview with
balconies.

Majori
Majori, 29 Jomas,
☎ 776 1380, Fax 722 1994
An excellent Art Nouveau building built in 1923 in the middle of
the village and 275yd (250m)
from beach. Friendly staff.

Lielupe
120 rooms.
Bulduri, 64/68 Bulduri Prospect,
☎ 775 2755, Fax 775 2694
Hotel 220yd (200m) from beach
with tennis courts, mineral water
indoor and outdoor swimming
pools and sauna.

Vaivari
80 rooms, 200 rehabilitation
rooms.
Vaivari, 61 Asaru Prospect,
☎ 776 6122, Fax 789 2705
A spa hotel with mud, thalassotherapy and medical consultations. It s also caters for rehabili-
tating children.

Jaunkemeri
200 rooms.
Jaunkemeri, 20 Kolkas
☎ 773 3267, Fax 773 1889
Situated in the furthermost village from Riga, the spa has a
good reputation.

INEXPENSIVE

Marienbade
150 rooms.
Majori, 43 Meierovica prospect,
☎ 776 2518, Fax 776 1464
One of the first spa hotels in
Jurmala, it has a good position
right on the sandy beach.
Seawater swimming pool, sauna,
gym and conference facilities in
addition to all the treatments.

Baltija
150 rooms.
Dzintari, 11 Dzintari prospect,
☎ 776 2138, Fax 776 2151
Spa hotel situated near beach

Zinatnes Nams
150 rooms.
Lielupe, 3 Vikingu,

☎ 775 1205, Fax 775 1234
A hotel located in a pine grove
550yd (500m) from the beach,
formerly a rest home for scien-
tists and near the station. It has
tennis courts, sauna, conference
facilities and water sports including yachting.

Jaundubulti Cottages
36 rooms.
Jaundubulti, 59 Dubulti prospect,
☎ 776 7045, Fax 776 7519
Simple accommodation in apartments including kitchen.

Daina
120 rooms.
Melluzi, 59 Melluzu prospect,
☎ 776 7057
Hotel with tennis courts, swimming pool, sauna, and all rooms
with balconies. Situated 220yd
(200m) from the beach.

Darta-A
Majori, 59 Juras,
☎ 776 2391, Fax 776 4420
A hotel near the beach with a
sauna.

Zvaigne
12 rooms.
Dubulti, 19 Meierovica prospect,
☎ 776 4681
A small quiet hotel near the
beach.

The Jurmala Spa and
Tourist Centre
Majori, 42 Jomas,
Jurmala LV-2015, ☎ 776 4276/
776 2167, Fax 776 4672,
E-mail jurmalainfo@mail.bkc.lv
A busy helpful office that offers
accommodation bookings as well
as general tourist information on
everything at the seaside.

CLIMATE IN LATVIA

Latvia has a temperate climate, which has considerable temperature variations. Summer is warm with long hours of sunlight, until mid-night during the solstice on June 23-24. Autumn and spring weather is mild while winter, which lasts from November to mid-March, can be extremely cold with temperatures below zero. Rain occurs throughout the year with the heaviest in August; snow is usual in winter.

For the weather forecast in English ring 711 2035 or check on the Internet www.meteo.lv

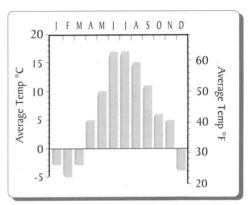

CONCERT HALLS AND OPERA HOUSES

Ave Sol
Hall of Chamber Music,
7 Citadel Street,
☎ 702 7547/702 7570

Dome Cathedral
1 Dome Square,
☎ 721 3498

Dzintari Concert Hall
1 Turaidas Street,
Jurmala,
☎ 776 2092, Fax 776 2086

Great Guild
Concert hall of the Philharmonic Society, 6 Amatu Street,
☎ 721 3798

Music Academy
1 K Barons Street,
☎ 722 3847

Opera House
Latvian National Opera,
3 Aspazijas Boulevard,

☎ 722 5803/722 8496,
Fax 722 8240,
E-mail admin@opera.lv.
Box office open 10am to 7pm.

Riga Congress Hall
5 K Valdemara Street,
☎ 732 3370

Riga Latvian Society
13 Merkela Street, ☎ 722 6881

St John's Church
7 Jan Street, ☎ 722 4028

St Peter's Church
19 Skarnu Street, ☎ 722 9426

Small Guild
3/5 Amatu Street,
☎ 722 3772/721 0093

Wagner Hall of Chamber Music
4 Richard Wagner Street,
☎ 721 0814/7

CULTURAL EVENTS

May	Lielais Kristaps, Big Kristaps Film Festival
June	National Opera Festival, Gadatirgus Arts & Crafts Fair at Ethnographic Museum
July	Rock Festival, Mezaparks
August	Sacred Music, Sudmalinas Folk Dance Festival

NB: As the actual dates of the events vary each year, it is prudent to pick up the monthly events guide on arrival or on Internet (see entry).

CURRENCY

The Latvian currency is the lat, which was introduced in 1993 and has remained stable since that time. The lat is divided into 100 santims, pronounced in a similar way to French centimes. Bank notes come in denominations of 5, 10, 20, 50 100 and 500 lats.

Banking hours are from 9am to 4pm, Monday to Friday. There are currency bureaux throughout the city and most restaurants and shops accept credit cards. Cash point machines are available at banks throughout the city and tourists need never be short of currency. German D-mark and US dollars are readily acceptable currencies, even by taxi drivers.

CUSTOMS REGULATIONS

The are no restrictions on importing or exporting hard currency.

The importing of pornography, arms, explosives or drugs is forbidden. Hunters who bring in their own weapons should have them cleared with the Ministry of Interior, 89 Stabu Street, ☎ 720 8618. A permit is required for the export of furs and animal trophies from the Forestry Department, ☎ 722 7057. Visitors who buy antiques or art are subject to a duty of 20 per cent for items 50 to100 years old and 10 per cent for over 100 years. Written permission is required from the Ministry of Culture, 22 Pils Street, ☎ 721 4100, open Monday, Tuesday and Thursday 2 to 4pm and 9am to 1pm on Wednesday and Friday. In most cases antique shops will arrange this for the purchasers.

For UK Residents

On entering Latvia, you are allowed one litre of alcohol, 200 cigarettes or 20 cigars or 200 grams of tobacco duty free.

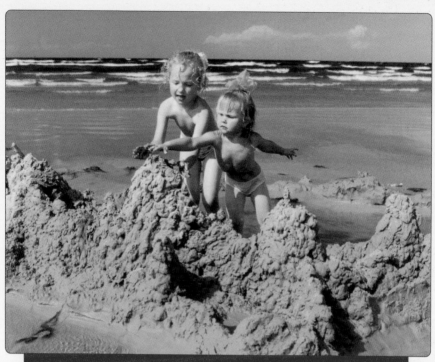

Above: Children enjoying beach life in Jurmala

Below: One of the finest examples of Art Nouveau in Jurmala, the Majori Hotel

Opposite: A perfect end to a perfect day

DIPLOMATIC CORP

Australia (Consulate)
3 Raina,
☎ 722 23 83, Fax 722 23 14

Canada
4 Doma Laukums, ☎ 783 01 41/
722 63 15, Fax 783 01 40

Ireland (Consulate)
54 Brívíbas (entrance from
Blaumana),
☎ 702 52 16, Fax 702 52 60

Israel
2 Elizabetes, ☎ 732 07 39/
☎ 732 09 80, Fax 783 01 70

UK
5 Alunána,
☎ 733 81 26, Fax 733 81 32

USA
7 Raina Bulv.
☎ 721 00 05, Fax 782 00 47

DRIVING INFORMATION

Driving is carried out on the right hand side of the road and the
speed limit varies from 31mph (50kph) in towns to 60mph (90kph)
outside.

On entering Jumala, all motorists are expected to pay one Lat, which
is a car tax. There are no parking meters in the area. Parking in the
Old Town of Riga is expensive, five Lats per hour. The roads vary in
quality so be careful of potholes. Petrol is cheap.

ELECTRICITY

The voltage in Latvia is the standard European 220 volts and if you
want to use an electrical appliance you will need an adapter as plugs
have twin points.

FLAG

The flag originated during a battle between the Latgallians and the
Knights of the Sword, in which the Latvians were victorious. Their
king was unfortunately seriously wounded and laid to rest on a white
sheet. After he died, his followers found that there was a parallel
stripe of blood either side of his body, while the area where his body
had been was miraculously untouched. They adopted it as their flag.

FLIGHTS

Riga is well served by major airlines and the airport (RIX) is only 4
miles (6.4km) from the city.

There are excellent connections from the US and Europe through
Lufthansa which flies via Frankfurt, **Air Baltic** and **SAS** via Copenha-
gen and Stockholm, **Finnair** via Helsinki, **British Airways** via
Heathrow, **Austrian Airlines** and **Lauda Air** via Vienna.

Airport (Lidosta)

Useful numbers

Information ☎ 720 7009/722 3305

2nd Floor (Book rooms for some hotels including airport Latavio Hotel, Russian style 8-11L)

Lost property	☎ 720 7236
Passenger Service	☎ 720 7935
Customs	☎ 720 7043, Cargo ☎ 720 7503
Immigration	☎ 720 7208
VIP Lounge	☎ 720 7132, Fax 720 7257

Airport Transfer

There are taxis as well as a regular bus service, number 22, from the Airport to the middle of the city. It only costs 18 santims and the journey takes about half an hour. The time taken by taxi is about 20 minutes and costs about 10 lats.

Riga Information (Arrivals level) ☎ 720 7800, Fax 720 7100. Also can provide accommodation.

Airline Offices

Air Baltic/SAS

The national airline together with SAS flies to 15 destinations including Helsinki, Tallinn, Moscow, Kiev, Minsk, Vilnius, Budapest, Warsaw, Prague, Frankfurt, Copenhagen, Stockholm, London, Zurich and Geneva.

Airport: ☎ 720 7401. City: 15 Kalku Street, ☎ 722 9166/6355. E-mail airbaltic@mail.bkc.lv

UK

It has five flights a day from London, the first at 06.50 for the early birds and the last at 16.00. The airline flies from three London airports, Heathrow, Gatwick and Stansted.

USA

It has excellent connections to the US and Canada to such cities as Calgary, Montreal, Toronto, New York, Seattle, Chicago, Washington, Atlanta, Miami and Los Angeles.

Austrian Airlines/Lauda Air

Airport, ☎ 720 7663, Fax 720 7668. City, 8 Kalku Street, ☎ 708 5070 721 6306/09. Helena Rudusa ☎ 920 9711.

UK

It has five flights a week from Heathrow via Vienna. If your flight arrives a day before your connection to Riga **Lauda** operates the

Like a *smile* in the SKY.

A network that embraces Central and Eastern Europe.

Austrian
Greats

The Kiss,
Gustav Klimt,
1907-8

Austrian Airlines Central and Eastern European network embraces 35 leading business cities within the region. No other carrier offers such a comprehensive service through a single hub. We operate frequent services to Vienna with excellent onward connections. Make Austrian Airlines your partner for business in Central and Eastern Europe and kiss goodbye to wasting time in transit. To find out more about our network contact your travel agent or visit our web site at: http://.aua.com

AUSTRIAN AIRLINES ➤

The Most Friendly Airline.

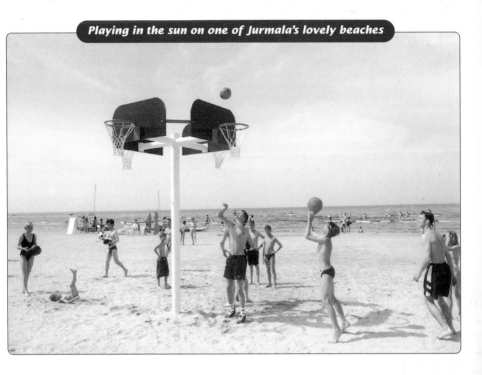

Playing in the sun on one of Jurmala's lovely beaches

Dzintari Station

'Vienna Impressions' program whereby, you get a free night's hotel accommodation.

USA

It has connections to the US to cities of New York, Washington and Miami. The 'Vienna Impressions' program operates on this route and provides you with a free night's accommodation if your connection is the next day.

British Airways

Airport, ☎ 720 7097. City, 4 Torna Street, ☎ 732 6737.

UK

Although it has a direct daily flight from Gatwick it is inconvenient for tourists going to Riga. It arrives near midnight, therefore you lose a whole day and it departs early in the morning around 07.00 so it leaves no extra time in the city.

Lufthansa

Airport, ☎ 720 7009, 720 7183/7381, Fax 720 7026.
City, 7-9 K. Baron Street, ☎ 728 5901, Fax 782 8199.

UK

There is one flight a week on a Saturday.

USA

There is one flight a day from Frankfurt and it has excellent connections from thirteen cities in the US and Canada including Vancouver, Toronto, Boston, New York, Philadelphia, Detroit, Chicago, San Francisco, Washington, Los Angeles, Atlanta, Dallas and Miami.

HEALTH

There are no reciprocal health agreements between the EU, UK or US, therefore medical and/or travel insurance is essential. No health certificates are required when visiting the country.

INTERNET INFORMATION

Latvian Web

Welcome to Latvia www.lv

Museums of Latvia vip.latnet.lv/LMA/
A site that has information on over 100 museums in Latvia. All are members of the Latvian Museum Association.

Hotels in Latvia www.itl.rtu.lv/CM/hotels.html
Information on many Latvian hotels with photos. Some hotels have on-line booking forms to book a room in advance.

Reactor Magazine www.reactor.lv
An on-line magazine about electronic music and related events in Latvia. DJ charts, popular party places, club schedules and radio broadcast schedules are among the information provided.

E-Lab www.re-lab.net
Art+Communications – that's the main slogan of E-Lab. This site provides information on many media art institutions – like Sounds OPEN Systems, Multimedia Center Riga, Latvian Academy of Arts and Latvian Artists' Union.

Latnet www.latnet.lv
Information provided by Latvian Academic Network.

LATNET Art Gallery www.gallery.lv/
Virtual gallery that welcomes all artists interested in collaboration with the gallery.

Riga This Week www.eunet.lv/Riga
A web page of a monthly events magazine.

Agency Riga 800 www.riga800.lv
A special agency established to celebrate the 800th anniversary of the founding of Riga. Provides information on events planned for 2001.

Riga in Your Pocket www.inyourpocket.com
A web page of a monthly events magazine.

Baltic Times www.lvnet.lv/baltictimes/artsent.htm
A website on news and current affairs.

MEDIA AND BOOKS

English and American newspapers and magazines are not readily available. There are a few outlets for English books, one of the best is **Globuss** at 26 Valnu Street and **Janis Roze** at 85a Elizabeth Street. *The Baltic Times*, a weekly newspaper, is a good way to be informed about the country.

NIGHTLIFE

There is an exciting and varied nightlife for all ages and visitors can watch cabaret or dance and disco until dawn. The added attraction is that the city is celebrated for the special beauty of its girls who are tall and statuesque and outnumber the men two to one.

The choice of nightclubs is wide and a small number only are mentioned.

The Admiral's Club

Has one of the best floorshows in town and comparisons have been made with the Moulin Rouge in Paris. The cuisine is Russian and after

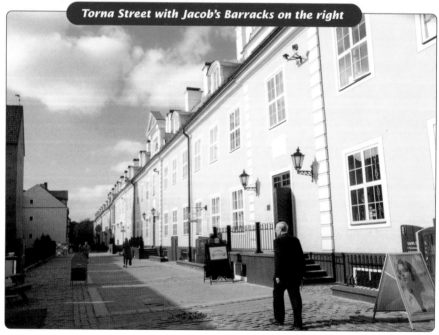

Torna Street with Jacob's Barracks on the right

Above: The Small Guild in Meistaru Street

Below: Footbridge over the canal

the show you can dance or play at the tables with minimum of chips as a casino is also part of the operation. There are three Admiral's Clubs, located at 12 Audeju, 8 Blaumana and 15 Marijas Streets.

The Mirage

Caters for the thirty-ish crowd and over, singles and couples, and has good floorshows. The nightclub is in the basement of the Riga Hotel on 22 Aspazijas Boulevard.

The Vernisage

This is a unique entertainment complex, which includes a disco, a piano bar, a musical theatre, a flower pavilion and a casino and is the brainchild of the famous pop singer Raymond Pauls. The disco is loud, smart, crowded and has a moving dance floor. The address is 2a Terbatas Street.

Cita Opera

Going to this club, which has live dance music on Fridays and Saturdays, is like being part of a big family because you are made welcome. The address is 21 Raina Boulevard.

Pepsi-Forums

For the young, up to 25 year-olds, and is for couples and singles. It is busy, crowded and has an up-to-date stage. Beware of the young Russian girls. You may get into trouble if you dance and flirt with them as they usually are accompanied by their boyfriends who just sit around. The address is 24 Kalka Street.

Underground

This is a place for teenyboppers, crowded and loud. Address is 1 Sloka Street.

Hamlets

A variety club that offers music, dancers and performances by actors and is run by the Latvian Actors Association. Address is 5 Jana Seta (on second floor).

Jazz

Live jazz, rock and blues is performed at an unusual venue of the former Reformed Church called **Dizzi Jazz Club**, 10 Marstalu, ☎ 721 0027.

Another interesting dance and jazz joint is **Pulkvedis** or **Nobody Writes to the Colonel** at 26/8 Peldu Street.

A young sophisticated French woman, Edith Uberle of Lufthansa was impressed with the nightlife as it had unique atmosphere and after dancing until dawn, she was able to unwind on the beach at Jurmala after breakfast.

People watchers need not go further than Kalku Street, which is the main promenade area of the city. There are throngs of people in the evening moving faster than the usual southern Mediterranean saunter.

Cafés

Visitors who prefer the café society rather than night clubbing also have a good choice as the city abounds in espresso bars.

The three places to go to feel the pulse of the city are M6, Osiris and Charleston's. **M6** in 6 Marstalu is frequented by the arty crowd and open until 11pm daily. You get an opportunity to take in an exhibition at the same time as the gallery is run by an artist's association. **Charleston** is the new trendy spot at 38/40 Blaumana Street to be seen and to see the talent. **Osiris** which is Zagars's creation has a good reputation for food and is a great place to have breakfast or brunch. It has got a continental atmosphere and you can sit for hours, reading the newspapers on display. It is at 31 Barona Street.

The café I prefer is called **Parliament** which is quiet, dignified and full of politicos or stockbrokers who talk in hushed tones. It has good Georgian wine and the address is 1/3 Smilsu Street.

The **Lolo Café** is the place for ladies that lunch and shop. A Viennese style café at 51 Elizabetes Street.

OPENING TIMES

The opening times for shops, museums and banks are similar to other European cities. Shops are open from 8am to 7pm and closed on Sundays. There are exceptions such as supermarkets Martini and Elida-L at 7 and 10 Grecinieku Street respectively; Interpegro at 33 Raina and Abolitis at 17 Barona.

Museums usually close on Monday but specific times are given in each case.

PASSPORTS/VISAS

Visitors from Ireland, UK, and USA do not require a visa to enter Latvia. Visas are required by visitors from Canada, Australia, New Zealand and Israel.

PHRASES

Hello, Hi!	*Sveiki*	OK	*Labi*
How are you?	*Ka iet?*	Thank you	*paldies*
Yes	*ja*	Please	*ludzu*
No	*ne*	Good morning	*labrit*

Aerial view of the Zeppelin hangars of the Central Market near the station

Good afternoon	*labdien*	Beer	*alus*
Good evening	*labvakar*	Open	*atverts*
Left	*Pa kreisi*	Closed	*slegts*
Right	*Pa labi*	Street	*iela*
Where?	*Kur?*	Square	*laukums*
When?	*Kad?*	Great Britain	*lielbritanija*
How much is it?	*Cik tas maksa?*	Pharmacy	*aptieka*
Do you speak English?	*Vai jus runajat angliski?*	Phone	*telefons*
		Doctor	*arsts*
I don't understand	*Es jus nesaprotu*	Flu	*gripa*
		Film	*filma*
Bill, please	*Rekinu, ludzu*	Bus	*autobus*
Have you film?	*Vai jums ir filma?*	Taxi	*taksometrs*
		Train	*vilciens*
I'm not well	*Nejutos labi*	Tram	*tramvajs*
Please call a doctor	*Ludzu, izsauciet arstu*	Airport	*lidosta*
		Ticket	*bilete*
Hotel	*viesnica*	Train Station	*dzelzcela stacija*
Bread	*maize*	Toilet	*tualete*
Coffee	*kafija*	Garage	*garaza*
Tea	*teja*	Petrol	*benzins*
Vegetables	*darzeni*		

POST

Post offices are open from 9am to 6pm on week days and from 9am to 1pm on Saturdays. The Central Post Office in Riga at 19 Brivibas (☎ 701 8700) is open 24 hours.

Post boxes are yellow and stamps for letters and postcards in Europe are 30 santims and 20 santims respectively and overseas airmail is 40 santims and 30 santims respectively.

PUBLIC HOLIDAYS

January 1	New Year's Day
April 2	Good Friday
April 4	Easter
May 1	Labour Day
May	Second Sunday in May is Mother's Day
June 23	Ligo or Midsummer Festival
June 24	O Jani or St John's day
November 18	Independence Day
December 25-26	Christmas and Winter Solstice
December 31	New Year's Eve

RESTAURANTS

Visitors are spoilt for choice, as there are many cheap restaurants. It is a city like Paris where you can eat well for little. Be adventurous and you will only spend a few lats on a meal. I have often done this at the Lido Bistros.

INEXPENSIVE

Lido Bistros
At 90 Brivibas, 54 Gertrudes, 65 Elizabetes and the Dome Square at 72a Mukusalas.
The bistros are run on a self-service basis. Besides a selection of salads, fruit and vegetable juices, barbecued meat, and fish, there is also beer.

Kekis
3 Kengaranga, ☎ 713 4930
Unpretentious Latvian food.

Alus Seta
6 Tirgonu, ☎ 722 2431
A rustic establishment, noisy and crowded which also has draft beer. A Lido clone.

Kirbis
1 Dome Square, ☎ 949 5409
A vegetarian menu with freshly squeezed juices. Self-service.

Pie Kuma
65 Caka, ☎ 229 8811
Ukrainian table with borsch and potato cakes.

Cita Opera
21 Raina Boulevard, ☎ 722 0770
A cellar bar and restaurant with music at weekends.

Divi Lasi
8 Tirgonu, ☎ 721 3470
Fish galore, including seaweed salad.

Arhitekts
4 Amatu, ☎ 722 6151
A hangover from Soviet times, this Russian restaurant is in the quintessential dark cellar.

Pizza Lulu
A pizza chain with outlets at 27 Gertrudes, 145 Valdemara, 55 Nometnu, Viada Petrol Station on Highway to Jurmala, ☎ 736 1234/936 1234.
Good pizzas and accessible too on internet: www.lulu.lv or 24 hours free delivery.

Staburags
55 Caka, ☎ 229 9787
Latvian fare served in ceramic saucepans in large portions.

MODERATE

Vermantis
65 Elizabetes Street, ☎ 728 6289
Argentinean steaks can be eaten at this Lido clone which has good views of Vermanes Park and rustic décor.

1739
6 Skarnu, ☎ 721 1398
Traditional Italian cuisine served in eighteenth-century house. Australian steaks and Hungarian paprika chicken also on the menu.

Aragats
15 Miera, ☎ 737 3445
A family-owned Armenian restaurant. Soup is a specialty and you can wash down your shashlik with ice cold vodka.

Mimino

78 Barona, ☎ 731 0641
A small place in a cellar with a brick fireplace. Try sand-boiled coffee and Georgian wine.

Grieku Restoraus

10/20 Skarnu, ☎ 721 1026
A Greek venture for Zagars, which lacks authenticity.

Sanhaja

26 Grecinieku, ☎ 722 8462
Seafood, sesame chicken, sweet and sour pork is available at this Chinese establishment.

Verdins

11 Maza Pils, ☎ 722 1339
French cuisine even bouillabaisse served in a secluded old Riga Courtyard.

Lielais Kamielis

3 Vecpilsetas, ☎ 721 2614
An unusual venue – a seven-teenth-century Warehouse. Try something heavy and typically Latvian like stewed pig's head with barley beans and peas.

Kalanda

8/10 Jana, ☎ 722 9775
A courtyard restaurant where you can taste Latvian specialties like Bull's testicles.

Boulevard No. 20

20 Aspazijas, ☎ 721 6033
A place for one of the best T-bone or sirloin steaks in the city.

Café Opera

3 Aspazijas, ☎ 721 1236
A good excuse to see the interior of the Opera House. Pre- and post-performance meals can be booked.

EXPENSIVE

When you need to impress a client or want to see the *Biezies* that come to these restaurants. The prices you will pay will be similar to places in the US and Europe.

Vincents

19 Elizabetes Street, ☎ 733 2634
Martins Ritins welcomes you in a white chef's outfit with red piping and red buttons. You can join all the celebs and even try the spinach salad which Prince Andrew ate and the special G&T that the Prince of Wales quaffed. The best quality Charolais steaks, guinea fowl and organic vegetables purposely grown for the restaurant.

The Symposium and the **New** or **Jaunais Restorans** are two fine examples of Zagars' cuisine and are both situated in Berga Bazaars, a new shop and apartment development off Elizabetes Street.

The Symposium

84/1 Dzirnavu, ☎ 724 2545
Known for its Mediterranean style cuisine. The new restaurant at 84 Dzirnavu, ☎ 721 7225 known for exotic meat and game like crocodile or ostrich medallions.

The Grill Room

At the Radisson SAS Hotel,
24 Kungu, ☎ 706 1111
The specialty is seafood and the chef Radek Cais has a creative flair.

Otto Schwarz
At Hotel de Rome, 28 Kalku,
☎ 708 7623
An over-rated and over-priced
restaurant with one of the best
views. A great place for a power
breakfast but be prepared to
operate the liquidiser yourself for
your carrot juice.

Piramida
At Park Hotel Ridzene, 1
Reimersa, ☎ 732 4432
A restaurant, at the plush, re-
cently renovated hotel, which is
on the ground floor.

At the seaside, Jurmala

Here you can eat well, particularly fish dishes, which are freshly
caught or smoked. A great place for a picnic is on the Talsu road,
about 15 minutes outside Jurmala where fishermen sell smoked fish.

MODERATE

Orient Sultan
Majori, 33 Jomas, ☎ 776 4473
Eastern European dishes as well
as fish are served in this popular
venue. It is the prime place to
watch promenaders.

At Gabriel's
Majori, 31 Jomas, ☎ 776 4268
An interesting Armenian menu.

Café de la Presse
Majori, 57 Jomas.
Open 24 hours during summer.
A wide selection of food includ-
ing barbecued dishes.

Haizivs & Bullis
Bulduri, 31 Bulduri, ☎ 775 3371
Surf and turf would have been
appropriate as a name rather than
Shark and Bull. Steaks served too
in its extensive menu.

Juras Zakis
Bulduri, 1 Viembas, ☎ 775 3005
Near the beach, and besides fish
dishes they have cheesecake for
dessert. Popular.

SHOPPING

The best buys are amber, linen and vodka. Latvia has been known
since ancient times as a supplier of amber, that remarkable translucent fossil gum from extinct coniferous trees which is trawled from
the sea during autumn, after storms. The range of amber varies from
many shades of brown to a light, milky white hue which is prized by
the locals. Some translucent amber is embedded with insects and as
a resin it is used for its curative properties. You can still find evidence
of how it occurred, as the coastline, even in Jurmala, has pine trees
growing on the edge of the beaches.

Linen is another traditional product as the country has long been a
producer of flax from which the fabric is woven. Bed linen and table-
cloths are popular, inexpensive items.

Vodkas are one of the best bargains and both plain and other varieties such as blackcurrant are available. The local company Latvijas Balzams produces its own brands such as Monopols, Rigas Originalis and Kristaldzidrais according to classic Russian technology as well as Stolichnaya. Its brands are organic as the company only uses grain, alcohol, water and sugar with no chemicals.

Incidentally, its other famous product is Black Balsam which is termed as a liqueur but originated from ingredients placed on wounds because of their excellent healing properties. It is used by the locals as a cold cure or in coffee and as a topping on ice-cream.

Other interesting souvenirs include handmade wooden toys, antiques, Soviet memorabilia, icons, leather goods and tinned sprats.

Souvenirs

A&E
17 Jauniela, ☎ 722 3200
The top shop for amber rings, necklaces, etc. Both Hillary Clinton and Helmut Kohl have bought items here.

Mara
9/11 Kaleju, ☎ 708 7541
Linen items available in many shades and a range of amber.

Sakta
32 Brivibas and 30 Azpazijas, ☎ 728 0868 and 722 7751 respectively.

General Souvenirs

St Peter's Church
There are many amber stalls behind the church.

Nordwear
1 Grecinieku, ☎ 722 5337
A range of handmade wool sweaters.

Antiques

Antiqua
20 Valdemara, ☎ 728 4377
A selection of art items.

Galerija
53 Dzirnavu, ☎ 728 2978
Soviet memorabilia.

Raritets
45 Caka, ☎ 227 5157
Icons, furniture, porcelain and paintings.

Volmar
39 Brivibas, ☎ 728 3436/
6 Skunu Street ☎ 721 4278
Paintings including recently discovered Latvian expressionist, Adolf Zardinsh, icons and silver.

Specialty shops

Globuss
26 Valnu, ☎ 722 6957
Established 40 years ago, this bookshop has a selection of English books as well as souvenir books on Latvia in English.

Avokado
60 Gertrudes, ☎ 728 8718
Herbs and spices.

Latvijas Bite
13 Gertrudes, 34b Dzirnavu and 1a Kalnina, ☎ 227 9495/722 6935 and 722 0001 respectively.
Honey from the Latvian Beekeepers Association.

Korkis
62 Avotu, 27 Blaumana and 8a Elizabetes, ☎ 724 3311 and ☎ 732 1130 respectively
Good selection of vodkas.

Sona Klets
28a Barona, ☎ 724 2398
Folk costumes.

Jana Rozes
83/85 Elizabetes, ☎ 728 6636/
5 Barona, ☎ 728 4288
Selection of maps and guide
books.

DANA K
187 Brivibas, ☎ 737 8618
A good selection of wooden
toys, models and household
articles.

TELEPHONES

The country has a modern digital telephone system. International
calls can be made either from hotels or phone booths with phone
cards. Country codes are as follows: UK (44), US (1), Canada (1),
Australia (61), Ireland (353), Israel (972).
   Emergency calls: Fire 01, Police 02, Ambulance 03.
   NB It is illegal to use a mobile phone while driving.

THEATRES

There are several theatres in the city but the works performed are
either in Latvian or Russian: **Dailes**, **Kabata**, **National**, **New Riga**,
Russian, **Drama**, **Skature** and **Hamlet Club**. There is also a **Puppet
Theatre**, 16/18 K. Barons Street, ☎ 728 5418 and the **Riga Circus**,
4 Merkela Street, ☎ 721 3472.

TIME ZONES

Latvia is GMT plus 2 hours.

TRANSPORT

Riga has a good, comprehensive public transport system that includes buses, trams, trolley buses and trains. It is cheap, costing
some 18 santims and tickets can be bought from conductors on
board with the exception of trains where they are purchased from
kiosks at stations. They run from 5.30am to 12.30am. Taxis are inexpensive too but use orange and black taxis with meters otherwise
you may have to haggle over the fare beforehand. For Jurmala, there
are regular train services from the Central Station or minibuses.

National and International Rail,
Bus and Ferry services

From the Central Station at Station Square, ☎ 723 3095, you can
reach Lvov in Poland, Moscow, St Petersburg, Vilnius in Lithuania and
Odessa. But check on journey times as trains are slow. Bus connections are widespread and destinations covered include Berlin,

LANDMARK VISITORS

(See page 175 for mailing details)

Cornwall*
ISBN: 1 901522 09 1
256pp, £10.95

Devon
ISBN: 1 901522 42 3
224pp, £9.95

Dorset
ISBN: 1 901522 46 6
240pp, £9.95

Somerset
ISBN: 1 901522 40 7
224pp, £10.95

Cotswolds
ISBN: 1 901522 12 1
224pp, £9.99

Hampshire
ISBN: 1 901522 14 8
224pp, £9.95

East Anglia
ISBN: 1 901522 58 X
224pp, £9.95

Scotland*
ISBN: 1 901522 18 0
288pp, £11.95

Jersey
ISBN: 1 901522 47 4
224pp, £9.99

Guernsey
ISBN: 1 901522 48 2
224pp, £9.95

Harrogate
ISBN: 1 901522 55 5
96pp, £4.95

GUIDES TO THE UK

Lake District*
ISBN: 1 901522 38 5
224pp, £9.95

Peak District
ISBN: 1 901522 25 3
240pp, £9.99

Yorkshire Dales
ISBN: 1 901522 41 5
224pp, £10.95

West Cornwall
ISBN: 1 901522 24 5
96pp, £5.95

South Devon
ISBN: 1 901522 52 0
96pp, £5.95

Southern Peak
ISBN: 1 901522 27 X
96pp, £5.95

Southern Lakeland
ISBN: 1 901522 53 9
96pp, £5.95

Dartmoor
ISBN: 1 901522 69 5
96pp, £5.95

New Forest
ISBN: 1 901522 70 9
96pp, £5.95

Isle of Wight
ISBN: 1 901522 71 7
96pp, £5.95

Hereford
ISBN: 1 901522 72 5
96pp, £5.95

Bremen, Brussels, Munich, Munster, Prague, Stuttgart as well as other Baltic states and Russian cities.

The ferry services are limited in schedules and only ply between Stockholm and Travemunde.

Car Rental Agencies include international companies like Avis, Hertz and Eurocar as well as local firms.

TOURIST INFORMATION

There are three main sources of information on the city and its environs:

Riga
Agency Riga 800
4 Torna Street, 1B-103 Riga LV-1050 Latvia,
☎ (371) 732 0550, Fax (371) 732 0609, www.riga800.lv

Old Town Centre
Riga LV 1050 Latvia, ☎ (371) 722 1731, Fax (371) 722 7680

Airport Riga Information
Riga LV-1053, ☎ (371) 720 7800, Fax (371) 720 7100,
E-mail tourinfo@lgs.lv

Airport Information
☎ (371) 720 7009/722 3305

City Council
3 Valdemara, Riga LV-1539, ☎ (371) 702 6177, Fax (371) 702 6337

Riga Seaside Resorts (Jurmala)
42 Jomas Street, Majori LV 2015, Jurmala, ☎ (371) 776 4276/2167,
Fax (371) 776 4672, E-mail jurmalainfo@mail.bkc.lv

Latvian Tourist Board
4 Pils Square, Riga LV-1050, ☎/Fax (371) 722 9945,
E-mail ltboard@com.latnet.lv, website www.latviatravel.com

Riga has a lively cultural life with music, theatre and opera and, in 2001, on its 800th anniversary, has been chosen as European City of Culture.

There are two sources of information on cultural events, the Information Centres and City Guides published monthly, such as *Riga This Week*, *Riga in Your Pocket* and *Riga Guide*.

BIBLIOGRAPHY

Agent's Manual 1999. Latvian Tourist Board (Riga 1998)

Art Nouveau Architecture of Riga. Riga 800 Jumava (Riga 1998)

Baedeker's Russia 1914. Baedeker (Leipzig 1914)

Baltic Outlook, March/April, May/June, August/September and October/November 1999

Benn, A & Bartlett, R, *Literary Russia*. Papermac (London 1997)

Einstein, Bergan R, *A Life in Conflict*. Little Brown (London 1997)

Bruders A, *Riga*, Madris (Riga 1997)

Byron, Robert, *The Road to Oxiana*. Picador (London 1997)

Dabolins, A, *Latvia*. Pluse Plus (Riga 1999)

Duncan, A, *Art Nouveau*. Thames & Hudson (London 1999)

Fahr-Becker, G, *Art Nouveau*. Konemann (I Koln 1997)

Feinstein, E, *Pushkin*. Phoenix (London 1998)

Freiberga, Vaira-Vike, *Acta Univeritatis Stockholmiensis – Studica Baltica Stockholmiensia 2*. 1985. Andrejs Pumpur's Lacplesis Stockholmiensia Journal of Baltic Studies

Handbook for Travellers. John Murray (1865)

Handbook for Travellers. John Murray (1893)

Hiden, J & Salmon, P, *Baltic Nations and Europe*. Longman (London 1994)

Jurmala This Week, Riga Guide

Kalnina, Dz, *English-Latvian Dictionary*. Avots (Riga 1997)

Kolbergs, A, *Riga*. Lauku Apgads (Riga 1993)

Kolbergs, A, *Story of Riga, Old Town and Parks and Boulevards*. Jana Seta (Riga 1998)

Krastins, J, *Riga Art Nouveau*. Metropolis Baltika (Riga 1998)

Lieven, A, *The Baltic Revolution*. Yale (London 1994)

Mandelstam, O, *The Noise of Time*. Quartet (London 1998)

Museums of Latvia. Latvian Museum Association Puse (Riga 1999)

Myers, A, *An Age Ago*. Penguin (London 1989)

Newman, E, *Life of Richard Wagner 1813-1848*. Knopf (New York 1966)

Noble, J, William, N & Gauldie, R, *Estonia, Latvia & Lithuania*. Lonely Planet (Hawthorn Australia 1997)

O'Brien, J, Ed New Latvian Fiction, *Review of Contemporary Fiction*. Illinois State (Normal US 1998)

Petersons, R & Naudis, A A, *Architectural Heritage of Jurmala*. (Jurmala Municipal Council 1998)

Radcliffe, M, *A Baltic Story*. R Radcliffe (London 1993)

Riga Downtown, Spring 1999 and Summer 1999

Riga In Your Pocket, Riga This Week

Silis, J, *Latvian-English Phrase Book*. Jumava (Riga 1996)

Tacitus, *The Agricola and the Germania*. Penguin (London 1970)

World Literature Today, Baltic Literature in the 1990s, Vol 72:2, Spring 1998

LANDMARK
VISITORS GUIDES

US & British VI*
ISBN: 1 901522 03 2
256pp, £11.95

Antigua & Barbuda*
ISBN: 1 901522 02 4
96pp, £5.95

Bermuda*
ISBN: 1 901522 07 5
160pp, £7.95

Dominican Republic*
ISBN: 1 90152208 3
160pp, £7.95

Pack 2 months
into 2 weeks
with your
Landmark
Visitors Guides

New Zealand*
ISBN: 1 901522 36 9
320pp, £12.95

Northern Cyprus
ISBN: 1 901522 51 2
176pp, £9.95

Orlando*
ISBN: 1 901522 22 9
256pp, £9.95

Florida: Gulf Coast*
ISBN: 1 901522 01 6
160pp, £7.95

Florida: The Keys*
ISBN: 1 901522 21 0
160pp, £7.95

St Lucia*
ISBN: 1 901522 28 8
144pp, £6.95

Provence*
ISBN: 1 901522 45 8
240pp, £10.95

Côte d'Azur*
ISBN: 1 901522 29 6
112pp, £6.50

Dordogne*
ISBN: 1 901522 67 9
224pp, £11.95

Madeira
ISBN: 1 901522 42 3
192pp, £8.95

Italian Lakes*
ISBN: 1 901522 11 3
240pp, £11.95

Bruges*
ISBN: 1 901522 66 0
112pp, £5.95

Iceland*
ISBN: 1 901522 68 7
192pp, £10.95

Ticino
ISBN: 1 901522 74 1
192pp, £8.95

Cracow*
ISBN: 1 901522 54 7
160pp, £7.95

India: Goa
ISBN: 1 901522 23 7
160pp, £7.95

India: Kerala
ISBN: 1 901522 16 4
256pp, £10.99

Sri Lanka
ISBN: 1 901522 37 7
192pp, £9.95

Prices subject to alteration from time to time

INDEX

For business and pleasure ...

the Radisson SAS has the best of both worlds!

The Radisson SAS Daugava Hotel is ideal for both business and pleasure! The Baltic's leading and largest conference hotel with 10 conference rooms for up to 360 people. The hotel features 360 fully equipped guest rooms, 53 Business Class rooms, fitness center and pool, salon, boutique shopping, casino, secure parking, fine dining, and superb views of the Old City. Complimentary transportation to and from the Riga Airport and also to the Old City. We are the only hotel in Riga offering SAS EuroBonus and Lufthansa Miles & More. Ask about our Romantic Weekend and Opera Weekend Packages!

100%
GUEST SATISFACTION
GUARANTEE
Radisson

Radisson SAS
DAUGAVA HOTEL RIGA
The difference is genuine.

24 KUGU STREET • RIGA LV-1048 • LATVIA • TEL:+371 706 1111 • FAX: +371 706 1100 • http://www.radisson.com